Hope When Shines Through

Compiled, Edited & Illustrated by

David Liverett

Hope
When
Shines
Through

David Liverett
Foreword by Christie Smith Stephens

Chinaberry House
P. O. Box 505
Anderson, Indiana 46015-0505
www.2lights.com

Cover: Painting by Ruthven Byrum
Back cover photography: Dale Pickett

ISBN 0-9632180-5-0
Printed in the United States of America

Dedication

To Connor Mark Liverett,
the light in his granddaddy's eyes

Foreword

When David Liverett and I were growing up in the 1950s in Austinville, Alabama, attending Sunday School, church services, Vacation Bible School at the Austinville Church of God, we learned many things about light and hope. Our teachers, pastors, and other folks in our community of faith taught us Bible verses, stories, hymns and choruses that shaped our minds and our souls. We memorized verses such as, "God is love," "Jesus wept," "In the beginning was the Word and the Word was with God and the Word was God," and "You are the light of the world." Inscribed upon our hearts were lyrics such as those penned by Charles W. Naylor, "God of light that illumes all space, God of glory and boundless grace." Lyrics such as those penned by William G. Shell, "Have we any hope within us of a life beyond the grave? We have a hope within our souls brighter than the perfect day." And choruses that little children around the world sang, "This little light of mine. I'm going to let it shine. Won't let Satan poof it out. Let it shine. Let it shine. Let it shine."

The Good Book more or less says, "Bring up a child in the way a child should go and the child when old will not depart from it." It has been awhile since David and I stood in the screen doorway of the Austinville Church of God on a Sunday night and saw the flames from the Dockerys' house on fire leaping up into the dark sky. But the fire, the passion of the Gospel, the light we saw when Brother Clarence Best was pastor, when my Aunt Mildred, David's mother Elna, my mother Pearl, Bonnie Poole, Sister Best, Mary Ellen Martin, and Jacquie Gross were our teachers, when my granddaddy and David's mama sang in the choir, when my daddy preached, my grandmother prayed, that passion we caught then still burns hot, leaps high within us today.

In the 1970s David and Avis and their son, Mark, lived in Maine. They love the North Atlantic coast and especially the lights that shine across the water, the lighthouses that have been salvation to people sailing on perilous seas. It was then that David's love for lighthouses was born and he took pen in hand to draw the light. Through the years he has gifted many of us with his lighthouse drawings. *When Hope Shines Through* is a treasure trove of his drawings of lighthouses from all over the United States and some from other countries as well. He has invited a number of his friends to write our thoughts and experiences about light and hope. The writings are as unique as the writers and all tell the good news of hope, "an anchor to the soul."

David Liverett, Artist, as surely as those hardy characters who tended these lighthouses, is a Keeper of the Light. He has light and hope within his soul and he won't let the "satans" of this world poof them out. This I know. Thank you, David, for your enduring friendship. Thank you for *When Hope Shines Through*. Thank you for lifting the lamp for us and for generations to come. Your mama and daddy are proud. Your family is proud. The sisters and brothers of Austinville Church of God and Park Place Church of God are proud. Miss Collier, Bobby, Carolyn and I and the whole second grade are proud. We all are grateful. God is smiling. My prayer is that light and hope will shine through every drawing and every word of this book. Shine on, Jimmy David. *When Hope Shines Through*, shine on.

Love, Emma Christie

Table of Contents

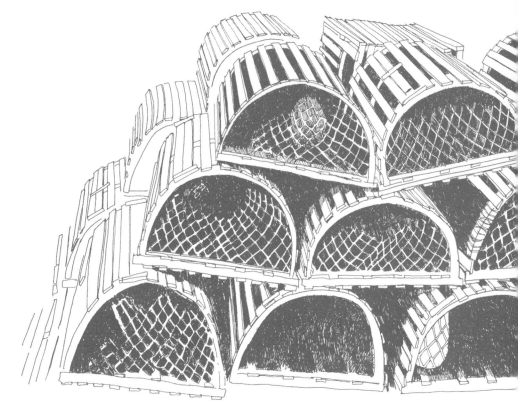

Introduction

One might wonder why bother publishing another book. If you enjoy going to any major bookstore or surfing the web, you know that many writers thought they could produce "the great American novel." I first became interested in the creation of books when I collaborated with my good friend, Christie Smith Stephens, in 1991. *Oh, to be in Miss Collier's class again!* tells about growing up in the 1950s in a small southern town.

In 1998 my wife and I made a trip to Prince Edward Island, Canada. After that trip I began drawing lighthouses again. I say *again* for I drew a series of lighthouses in the mid 1970s when my family lived in Cape Elizabeth, Maine. With no particular motive in mind, I spent the next year completing over thirty pen and ink illustrations. Still with no clue of a book in the future, the thought came to me about a series of lighthouse greeting cards. Later, a book seemed to be more practical to produce, but that meant more lighthouse drawings. If I could draw one hundred and find scriptures and hymns that speak of rescuing and finding peace, that might be the basis for an inspirational book.

For me, what happened Labor Day Weekend, 2000, was clearly an inspired event. My friend, Roscoe Snowden, spoke in church on the subject of "hope." His scripture reference was Hebrews 6:19. *"We have this hope as an anchor for the soul, firm and secure."* I began thinking that if I could get one hundred of my friends to write about hope and/or light, I might have the manuscript I needed.

This didn't sound like such a large task since I knew many good writers. Those who contributed come from a variety of backgrounds and geographical localities. Many are from the Midwest, while others hail from Maine, Florida, Wyoming, Texas, and California and even as far away as Japan and Lebanon. These unique individuals span several generations from a present university student to an elder statesman in the church who is ninety!

It has been a joy and privilege to work with each contributor. Their stories have awed, inspired and humbled me. It has been a special blessing to read their words and realize that some have honored a loved one on these pages. To each of you I give my heartfelt thanks and appreciation for your willingness and gracious acceptance of this task. Without you, my dream of this publication would never have been realized.

In 1974 I drew my first lighthouse. Cape Elizabeth Lighthouse "Two Lights" *Built in 1874* Cape Elizabeth, Maine

My wife, Avis, has gone beyond the call of duty with this project and I want to thank her for her love and patience. My assistant, Tamara Burrell, has used her technical expertise to achieve the desired results for this book and I thank her as well. The proofreading efforts of Harry Hudson, Jan Slattery, Wayne Gordon, and Christie Stephens are much appreciated. Many thanks also to those who provided photographs for drawing lighthouses I have not yet seen.

The cover of this book comes from a painting by Ruthven Byrum (1896-1958). Although I never met him, he has inspired me to be the best that I can be. Mr. Byrum painted the lighthouse at Cape Neddick, Maine, in the 1940s and it is one of my favorites. This painting has hung in my studio for almost twenty years. It is a reminder of the man who began the art department at Anderson University, the school where I received a degree in art and where I taught for many years.

David Liverett
February 22, 2001
Anderson, Indiana

Flesh of Flesh Spirit of Light

For Arthur Duell and Wayne Gordon
Uncle and Nephew

Tall like a Fir tree
with ocean-large hands
he's one-of-a-kind
a broke-the-mold original
citizen of the earth
the quintessence of will.

Golden Pioneer
whose chosen hermitage
rests by the woods
where deer appear
and keep company.

Jack-of many-trades
veteran of the big war
builder of his own boats
once upon a time
three a year
catcher of fish
polisher of rocks
Tiger Eyes Thunder Eggs
Apache Tears he finds
on this land—his Eden
this Oregon.

Seafarer alone on the Pacific
eight miles out when

pea soup fog envelops
all sight obscured
no light to show the way
no light flashing piercing
pointing protecting leading.

Seafarer alone on the Pacific
eight miles out
shrouded in thick gray
visibility zero
seafarer captain
inventor of survival
prepared prepared
always be prepared.

In his possession
a transistor radio
in his possession knowledge
experience on the waters
wisdom perseverance
a calm in the possible doom.

Radio he turns on
pulls out the antenna
knowing the location of the
stations on land on shore

Continued on page 16

Cape Elizabeth Lighthouse "Two Lights" *1874*
Cape Elizabeth, Maine

he points points points
locating the strongest signal
turns his hand-crafted ark
toward the voice that offers harbor
the song that sings of safety
the word that speaks of hope
the air waves of life.

Seafarer wayfinder wilderness one
does not travel in unending circles
tunes his ear to sounds rescuing
hears his way home.

Devoid of sight
he is as is written
The Light.

In his own way inimitable
he keeps the wild light
refusing to be conquered by
elements of so-called civilization
like his green now mostly rust
1957 Willys "Jeep" setting in the
nature-groomed untamed yard
He is *Not For Sale*.

He lifts the lamp of freedom
sings the songs of liberty
for all who have the courage
to see and to hear
to create their own vessels

to chart their own courses
to listen for
to tune in to
unusual sounds of salvation
to make/find their/our own ways
to sing along with him—

> *The wind blows by me*
> *The wind blows free*
> *The wind blows by me*
> *The wind blows free*
> *It blows right past me...*

Arthur Duell as a young man

Christie Smith Stephens
March, 1999, from stories told to me by Wayne Gordon

Cape Meares Lighthouse *1890*
near Tillamook, Oregon

Stuck in the Muck

A few years ago a barge sank in the New York harbor. It settled in the Hudson River bottom and became embedded in the mud. The owners surveyed the mess wondering what to do about that expensive piece of equipment stuck in the muck. Gigantic floating cranes were brought in. Efforts were made to raise and salvage the barge, but the mud sucked on it, clinging to it like glue, and it couldn't be budged. No human device had enough power, it seemed, to hoist it out of the mire.

Then a tugboat captain came up with a bright idea. He ordered deep-sea divers to attach many cables to the sunken vessel. At low tide the ends of the cables were fastened to several tugboats and the slack tightened. When the tide began to rise, the power of the Atlantic Ocean itself began relentlessly to buoy up the various tugs until finally the sunken barge was pulled free of the river bottom and slowly raised to the surface.

Our lives can become as mired in the muck of depression and despair as that barge was in the river bottom. When that happens human efforts alone are often useless. We hear stories almost daily of people, attempting to cope with devastating circumstances through human resources alone, knowing only resentment and bitterness. At the same time we are aware of people of faith, while grieving and sad, knowing joy through accepting God's healing grace.

We can see a pattern emerging. Only the hope inspired by the promises of the Bible—which are backed by the irrepressible strength of God's power—can pull us loose and bring us to the surface.

What could keep you and me stuck in the mud: grief? anger? holding a grudge? withholding forgiveness from a friend or loved one? envy? self imposed pity party? We have a choice. We can remain mired or we can be buoyed by the strong cords of God's power through His love and grace. With the Psalmist, we find there's always hope in that.

John L. Albright

"I waited patiently for the LORD; he turned to me and heard my cry. He lifted me out of the slimy pit, out of the mud and mire; he set my feet on a rock and gave me a firm place to stand. He put a new song in my mouth, a hymn of praise to our God..."
—Psalm 40:1-3

A Whistling Buoy

Cape Porpoise, Maine

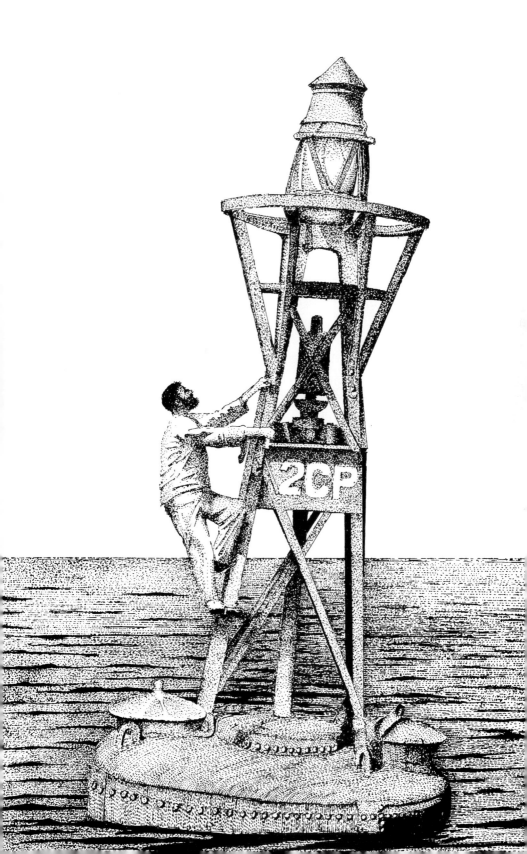

Is There Any Hope?

During World War II the submarine, *U.S.S. Squalus*, was returning to the Portsmouth, New Hampshire, Navy yard when its power failed and it sank in the harbor. Rescue ships hurried to help, and many other ships "stood by." Divers found the sunken ship mired in the bay bottom. They communicated with the captain by pounding with heavy hammers on the hull of the ship, using the dot-dash of the Morse code.

After long exchanges of data, the crew began to tap another message: "Is there any hope?" Millions heard the story by radio. I remember driving across the bridge and looking out to the ships trying to get help to trapped seamen. I know many did as I did. We prayed as we waited and waited. The rescuers used a new device called the Momsen Lung and finally were able to rescue all the crew members.

What a question—Is there any hope? Who of us at some time has asked the same question. It is universal, for all of us sometimes are trapped like the *Squalus*. For the Christian the firm answer is YES. That is the core of the Christian faith. There is hope for every "hopeless" situation. Christ, the hope of the world, stands beside you now to rescue and to work redemptively for your good.

Back to Portsmouth Harbor...Later the *Squalus* was raised, repaired and re-commissioned for more active service. Hope was not in vain, nor is it for you and me. Christ is our hope.

T. Franklin Miller

"To them God has chosen to make known among the Gentiles the glorious riches of this mystery, which is Christ in you, the hope of glory."
—Colossians 1:27

Alcatraz
Island
Lighthouse
1909

San Francisco,
California

My Lighthouse

You are my lighthouse—my city set on a hill.
When my life-compass is shattered or lost,
your constant light of love brings me back on course.

You are my lighthouse
when disappointments weigh like an anchor on my spirit
and the light of your song sets me free.

You are my lighthouse
when the heavy fog of confusion settles deep in my mind
and the light of your wisdom brings rays of
understanding.

You are my lighthouse
when winds of disease rip through my body
and the light of your smile calms my sea of fear.

"You are the light of the world. A city on a hill cannot be hidden. Neither do people light a lamp and put it under a bowl. Instead they put it on its stand, and it gives light to everyone in the house."
—Matthew 5:14-15

You are my lighthouse
when I am drowning in the dark sea of depression
and the light of your strength reaches down and pulls me
out.

You are my lighthouse
when the waves of grief break over my heart
and the light of your quiet presence helps me ride out
the storm.

You are my lighthouse
when the waters are calm and the sailing smooth
and the light of your friendship brings joy to my journey.

Life is a voyage from one shore to another,
but we are never on our own because
you are my lighthouse and I am yours.

Point Montara
Lighthouse
1928

San Francisco,
California

Dedicated to the "lighthouses" of the Park Place
Truthfinders Sunday School Class

Ilene Gray Bargerstock

Root of Hope

Point Cabrillo
Lighthouse
1909

near Mendocino,
California

Hope! Is there one word used more often in daily conversation that conveys so many meanings? "I hope to see you again" or "I hope you do well on your final exams" is hope as expectation. Often it implies a wish: "I hope you will be happy in your new job." In an attempt to encourage someone who has faced repeated failures a friend might say, "Hang in there, you can always hope that you will succeed with your next try." *Hope, like the gleaming taper's light adorns and cheers our way: And still as darker grows the night, emits a brighter ray.* —Oliver Goldsmith from *The Captivity*

The Hebrew word for hope is *tikvah* which stems from a root meaning "hopefully waiting." One learns to wait for release from problems and pain, not a resigned waiting or a despairing waiting, but expectant waiting. The National Anthem of Israel is titled *Hatikvah* meaning "The Hope." A free translation of a part of the lyrics is: *'Tis not yet lost, our hope to be free people in our land.*

A friend of mine watched his twelve year old daughter die as the result of a rare blood disease. He shared a copy of the sermon he used at her memorial service. He described the valleys and the mountaintop experiences the family shared during the long struggle with treatments and transfusions, and finally merciful death. Through it all the family shared a growing bond of love and hope beyond this life. They were strengthened in their appreciation for each other, and faith in an all wise God and His ultimate will and purpose for them and their daughter. They found Hope!

As the lighthouse towering above the waves brings a sense of direction and assurance to a lost sailor, so hope causes one to look up and accept the peace God is waiting to give. Hope does not mean God will fix the problem, but will help us find an acceptance and understanding plus the inner resources that bring strength to ride out the storm.

Roscoe Snowden

Lead, Kindly Light

"Look to the light! Look to the light," came the fearful cries of early sailors as their ship entered the darkened shoals of an unknown sea.

Sitting on a hill far across the waves stood the lonely sentinel flashing its beacon of light across the waters. The lighthouse, standing guard over the treacherous reefs and shallows, providing safe passage for a ship in need.

For centuries, the lighthouse was a saving light to so many mariners who ventured forth into the world's waters. As early as 750 BC, Homer, an epic poet of Greece, recorded a tribute to the lighthouse in *The Iliad*:

> *"So, to night-watering sailors pale with fear*
> *Wide o'er the watery waste a light appears,*
> *Which on the far-seen mountain blazing high*
> *Streams from lowly watchtower to the sky."*

Many writers through the years have used the symbolism of the lighthouse and its saving light, likening it to God, our Father, the Light of the world.

In similar ways, God's holy light is here to save us. It gives us guidance through life's treacherous journey and it provides assurance and comfort to our fears. But we, too, must look to the light! We are warned: *"...you will do well to pay attention to it, as to a light shining in a dark place, until the day dawns and the morning star rises in your hearts."* —II Peter 1:19

One of the world's most beloved hymns, penned by John Henry Newman, has inspired countless thousands to look to the light.

> *"Lead, kindly light...the night is dark,*
> *and I am far from home.*
> *Lead thou me on."*

Cleda Achor Anderson

"...you will do well to pay attention to it, as to a light shining in a dark place, until the day dawns and the morning star rises in your hearts."
—II Peter 1:19

Egmont Key
Lighthouse
1858

near
St. Petersburg,
Florida

26

Waves of Immortality

Hence, in a season of calm weather
Though inland far we be,
Our Souls have sight of the immortal sea
Which brought us hither,
Can in a moment travel thither,
And see the children sport upon the shore,
And hear the mighty rolling waters evermore.

William Wordsworth
from *Ode, Intimations of Immortality*

Inlanders
are oft removed from the power of the sea,
fail to remember the immensity of the deep,
hurricane fierceness, density of fog,
peril of the swell, largeness of jagged rocks,
absence of light, relief of harbor,
but only need connection to
our close brushes with death,
clinchings of the chest,
involuntary holdings of breath,
awakenings in the dark,
to relate ever so knowingly
to the seafarer's small boat cast on ocean vast,
to claim these more than metaphors as our own.

And on that pacific day in sunlight rejoice
with Wordsworth and the sporting children
traveling hither/thither evermore
on waves of immortality.

Christie Smith Stephens

"Peace I leave with you; my peace I give you. I do not give to you as the world gives. Do not let your hearts be troubled and do not be afraid."
—John 14:27

Cana Island
Lighthouse
1869

near
Baileys Harbor,
Wisconsin

28

Symbol of Hope

The wind was definitely picking up. Even before I heard the weather advisory, I knew this typhoon was going to be stronger than many we'd experienced in Japan. I'd been out with a friend, but her little car had been buffeted by such powerful gusts of wind that we decided we'd better go home. And then the banging began.

It sounded like the roof of the shed. But when I looked out the kitchen window, I saw that the roof was still nailed securely. Still, the banging continued—like the report of a gun—with every strong blast of wind. Finally, braving the storm, I went outside to investigate. To my dismay, I found that the back of the lean-to had come loose. The real danger was that the heavy wooden wall would completely break off and become airborne. If this happened, it would likely damage the neighbor's closely situated house. I had to do something, and quickly.

Struggling to stay on my feet in the wind, I looked around frantically, wondering what was the answer to this emergency that had caught me at home without my husband. The sight of the sturdy maple tree in our yard calmed and reassured me. I would tie the back wall of the shed to the tree by securing a heavy rope to the inside crossbeam. With the maple tree anchoring the lean-to, the typhoon passed safely.

That maple tree is my symbol of hope—hope whose name is Jesus Christ. He is the strong anchor of my life that keeps me safe and secure. Always. No matter the place. No matter the storm.

Cheryl Johnson Barton

"We have this hope as an anchor for the soul, firm and secure..."
—Hebrews 6:19

Point Loma Lighthouse
1855

San Diego, California

30

Blazing Radiance

Have you experienced the spiritual stimulation found in the great cathedrals of Europe? Their architectural designs are intended to convey powerful images of Christian faith. The builders put their vision of reality into the magnificence of glass and stone. For the spiritually hungry, seekers can encounter in these magnificent places the mystery of God and resources for the journey of faith. Here are Christian messages now frozen in structures dedicated to God.

These stunning buildings are giant crosses when seen from the air. The death and resurrection of Jesus are central. The all-enveloping space within the cross design suggests the safety and wisdom of an expectant mother. The church nurtures believers and is a shelter of peace and divine presence, the family of God, the ark of Noah during the floods of life.

The use of light is symbolic of the Christian pilgrimage. On first entering a Gothic cathedral, one is plunged into near darkness. The eyes struggle to adjust. The message? We all come to Christ and God's people as sinners, lost and blinded. We must become aware of our lostness, how dark it is within, how in need of God's grace we are. The cathedrals force us into the shadows before we are introduced to light. Finally, one encounters the blazing radiance of a rose window that takes the breath away.

God's grace is welcome light. It is made vividly plain that Christ was rejected and suffered on our behalf. That is the darkness Jesus accepted for us. But made plain also is that *"...light shines in the darkness, but the darkness has not understood it."* —John 1:5 As we move about in the magnificent resurrection light of the inner cathedral, grace abounds and new life waits. We are beckoned to receive the light and then go out into the world to let the light shine!

Barry L. Callen

"The light shines in the darkness, but the darkness has not understood it."
—John 1:5

Point Pinos
Lighthouse
1855

Monterey,
California

Hope and Light

Hope is as necessary to life as light and air. This is particularly true since we live with contradicting actualities. When our emotions are controlled or influenced by events, hope alone remains buoyant. Hope brings light to the situation.

Recently, I walked through the dark halls where there was illness and those who have grown older are confined. My thoughts drifted. Does hope come when the light comes on? Or does hope cause the light to burn brightly? As Forrest Gump might say, "Maybe it is a little of both." Yes, a little of both for those gallant persons on journeys with painful contradictions.

Here are some words recently penned by a person on her Christian journey. She represents many of us in our search for that often elusive hope.

> *Hope is a well*
> *Its sides are formed by rock;*
> *It's grounded over a spring*
> *Flowing from the river of peace.*
> *Its dipping rope has no end*
> *Its cup runs over with living water.*
> *Burdens tossed in become weightless.*
> *Sins fall below its depths and*
> *Prayer petitions float at its surface,*
> *To be transcended to heaven on the*
> *Golden rays of the sun.*
>
> (*Barbara Mahini,* with permission*)*

Today, visit the well again. Jesus is always at the well. And when you desperately need direction and meaning you will find light for your journey. Hope will fill the moment with steadfast faith. Or is it that faith fills the moment with hope and light? Come and celebrate. You will not be taken out of this world, but provided direction and power for the ordering of life in the present.

James W. Bradley

"...I am the light of the world. Whoever follows me will never walk in darkness, but will have the light of life."
—John 8:12

"Now faith is being sure of what we hope for and certain of what we do not see."
—Hebrews 11:1

St. Augustine
Lighthouse
1874

Anastasia Island,
Florida

The Light at the End of the Tunnel

I have always been mildly claustrophobic. Such things as tight turtlenecks, rings, hard to unlatch seat belts and very crowded elevators tend to bother me. Sometimes they can create a mild panic state.

A test of my claustrophobia came a few years ago when I had the opportunity to go through Hezekiah's Tunnel in Jerusalem. This five hundred and ninety-seven yard long, shoulder-wide, almost head-high, very dark tunnel carved out of solid rock is filled with fast flowing water from knee to waist deep its entire length. It took lots of self-talk to even agree to enter the tunnel and even more to appear relatively calm to my four fellow explorers, especially when about halfway through my small flashlight went out. I tried to assure myself that there had been no earthquakes in this area for hundreds of years and that I had heard nothing about a terrorist attack, cave-in or drowning in recent history. There were no yard markers or other indicators of the distance to the exit. Finally after what seemed like an eternity, I began to see some faint light indicating "the end of the tunnel." I thanked God for the bright light of His sunshine and for giving me the opportunity and "courage to survive" this experience.

About a year ago, Anita, my wife of forty-two years, suffered a brief but fatal illness and I experienced the dark tunnel of grief and loneliness. I am now engaged to be married in a few months and I am seeing the light at the end of the tunnel of aloneness. I find it interesting that many people who have near-death experiences describe going through a tunnel-like darkness into a dazzling light. Ultimately, there *is* light and hope at the end of the tunnel.

Joe K. Womack

"Light is sweet, and it pleases the eyes to see the sun."
—Ecclesiastes 11:7

Boca Grande
Lighthouse
1932

near
Boca Grande,
Florida

36

Hope in the Unseen

Historic lighthouses have guided many a ship to safety through a beacon of light across the waves. How needed were these lights and how dedicated were the keepers. Lighthouses now serve us as icons of hope, symbols pointing to a security far more trustworthy. We have a hope, an invisible but real light that shines through the darkness. Jesus, the Christ, is that light, the life and hope of the world.

I served in the U.S. Navy during World War II. Our ships trusted in a more secure guidance system, an unseen beam never hindered by clouds or storms. This signal guided us. I remember a time when a typhoon with a hundred and fifty mile winds hit the western Pacific Ocean. Dark clouds, winds and rain blinded our visibility. Walls of water pounded the decks of our ship. Waves as high as fifty feet on one side and as low as fifty feet on the other side almost turned us over. As we plowed into the waves and winds an unseen beacon guided us. Prayers went up, caution was observed and, yes, we were thankful for guidance. However, the equipment for receiving that beam had to be kept ready and watchmen had to be alert, just as did watchmen on older sailing ships. We trusted the equipment and the operators. An unseen beacon kept up our hope. We did not know the specifics but we knew the source.

We Christians have an unseen light of hope. In the Bible faith claims specifics but hope trusts in God for what He sees best. Though unseen, we trust in God's unspecified promises, a hope both steadfast and sure. God does provide!

God, keep our hope in you for the days ahead and for eternity. A-men.

W. Malcolm Rigel

"For in this hope we were saved. But hope that is seen is no hope at all. Who hopes for what he already has? But if we hope for what we do not yet have, we wait for it patiently."
—Romans 8:24-25

Copper Harbor
Lighthouse
1866

Copper Harbor,
Michigan

The Perfect Storm, 59 A.D.

You do not have to be a sailor to find the story of Paul's shipwreck exciting. Imagine yourself aboard. Feel the torrential wind. Grab onto something solid before you wash overboard. Swallow some water.

Paul is being taken as a prisoner to Rome. A hurricane-force storm called a *nor'easter* drives their ship out into the Mediterranean. They do everything they know how to do to control the ship. They take increasingly desperate actions. Their frantic attempts to save themselves are based on false hopes...

Years ago, I taught a Junior High Sunday School class session on hope. I asked the kids if they could tell me the difference between false hope and genuine hope. A student answered quickly, "False hope comes from us. Real hope comes from God."

When the leaders on the ship run out of ideas, options, courage, they run out of hope. They cannot trust "hope that comes from us." Verse twenty marks the turning point in the story. *"When neither the sun nor stars appeared for many days and the storm continued raging..."* Their navigational reference points are gone. *"We finally gave up all hope of being saved."* They focus on real and imagined dangers and give up hope. They are drifting thirty-six miles per day. They know it's a matter of time before they crash into something. By the end of the story, they have been in hurricane weather for six hundred and twenty-five miles and their ship is wrecked. The last line tells the happy ending: *"...everyone reached land in safety."*

Have you ever experienced times of hopelessness? Reference points gone. Anxiety about dangers, real and imagined. Fear for your life. If you came to experience real hope, did you recognize it as a gift from God?

When we give up our false hopes, it is just as well. Then, when God does help us, we can recognize our divine deliverance for what it is.

James R. Cook

"When neither sun nor stars appeared for many days and the storm continued raging, we finally gave up all hope of being saved. After the men had gone a long time without food, Paul stood up before them and said...'I urge you to keep up your courage, because not one of you will be lost...'"
—Acts 27:20-22

Tybee Island Lighthouse
1867

near Savannah, Georgia

The Middle Bay Cow

Whenever I write a cow always seems to appear bringing a story, a lesson holy.

A cow such as the one in my workbook when I was child in elementary school, the cow whose directions I failed to follow, the cow who taught me the lessons of shame, of imperfect perfection, the lesson of the preciousness of children, the lesson of the necessity for freedom in art.

A cow such as the one kept by E.E. Byrum in the Trumpet commune long after other folks had moved beyond the keeping of livestock, had moved past such symbolic realities of yesteryear. The Trumpet Cow who taught me lessons of a cherished heritage, of the problems, pressures, privileges of living in community, lessons of moving on...

A cow such as the one Granddaddy Toon had on his farm when I was a little girl, the cow whose tit Jerry lifted and shot unpasteurized milk into my mouth, the cow who taught me that before milk is cold it is warm, lessons of surprise and laughter.

And now on this lighthouse journey a cow appears on the porch of the Middle Bay Lighthouse, a Chesapeake style, setting in the middle of Mobile Bay, Alabama. From shore I can't see this lighthouse although Jim Gray's watercolor and David's pen and ink drawing have secured it in my mind's eye, Middle Bay Lighthouse looking like a large crab guarding the waters and the shoreline.

It was Adam Pope who told me about the cow of Middle Bay Light. He saw her in the story told down generation to generation. Adam's family has owned the restaurant on the Fairhope pier for years. He grew up in this place, was reared in its light. This is home. He loves its beauty. He loves its stories.

Adam said that once upon a time the keeper of Middle Bay Light had a cow, a cow kept on the porch of this unusual home halfway up Mobile Bay past Sand Island Light, past Mobile Point Light and before you got to Battery Gladden or Choctaw Point. It was a time before electricity, at least before electricity in the middle of water, a time before refrigeration. The keeper kept a cow so that there could be milk to drink, milk to cook with, milk to nurture, to build strong bones.

Continued on page 44

Middle Bay Lighthouse *1885*
near Mobile, Alabama

Why do I so love Adam Pope's story about the cow and the lighthouse? I suppose because it challenges my thinking about what is possible. It is difficult enough for me to imagine living out in the middle of the water especially during a storm, hurricanes come through here from time to time, living so isolated although that has a primal appeal. It is hard to think about tending the light, being responsible for the safety of folks through the night, helping those lost or in trouble even though I have a natural inclination for missionary work. But add to that the need to care for a cow in such limited space and the questions overtake me. How did this cow get here? Where is this cow's food kept?

I can see that cow pacing round and round, fenced in. I can see the keeper shoveling the deck and sitting on a three-legged stool placing a tin bucket under the udder. I can hear the first squirts hitting the bottom of the bucket, percussion foaming, cream later rising, butter churned with a wooden paddle in a crock like my mama used when she was growing up on the farm.

I love this story because so little fact creates so much thought, wonder and relationship among strangers.

The keeper, the cow and the light that save, nourish and cause me to laugh just thinking about a cow on a porch of a lighthouse. I milk it for all it's worth and then some, learn the lessons that shine across water, time and across the limits of the mind.

I stand on the shore on a clear night and I can see an old keeper drinking a glass of milk while a cow jumps over the moon. Somewhere in the dark a little dog laughs. There is a dish and spoon contemplating an exit. A child quotes the lines of nursery rhyme. Such sport—

Let there be stories.
Let there be cows.
Let there be children.
Let there be imperfection.
Let there be art.
Let there be cherished heritages.
Let there be community.
Let there be family.

Let there be warm surprises.
Let there be strangers telling tales.
Let there be milk.
Let there be strong bones.
Let there be laughter.
Let there be keepers.
Let there be light—

So be it.

Christie Smith Stephens

 Sand Island Lighthouse *1873*
near Fort Morgan, Alabama

End of Summer

I think of the end of summer as a time of anticipation —anticipation of new possibilities, new jobs, new relationships, new things. However, for me the end of summer that year brought not anticipation but a crescendo of whispering voices. Those voices ignited within me my deepest levels of inadequacy and fear of failure.

That was surface stuff. Underneath it all was a deep question about my survival this time. Yes, I had learned the skills of work survival. But I had also discovered that the drive for survival had many times left me alienated and alone. Self-reliance had taught me well the lessons of just a little more, just a little harder. But that just a little more many times had driven me away from God and significant others who didn't want me to be alone in my self-reliance.

Because of a new, emerging awareness of God's genuine interest in my life and desire to give good things to me, I genuinely wanted to respond to the current crisis in a different way. So, of all the crazy things, I felt compelled to begin reading again in the minor prophets! Granted, these fellows are not commonly seen as the sure source of inspiration and encouragement. When I got to the final chapter of Hosea one sentence seemed to leap off the page and pierce its way into my understanding and heart. The Lord speaks in such a succinct manner and answers the implied question, "Who in the world do you think I am, Joe?" with *"I am the one who answers and looks after you."*

"I look after you." Those words anchored in my thoughts, spilled over in my emotions—to think that if God said he looks after me I am really looked after! Failure did not matter so much, nor did what people might think or what contingency plans may have to be put in place. God was looking after the whole mess and He said He would answer. I discovered that the light of those words dispelled my aloneness and would bring incredible hope for the intense days ahead.

Joseph L. Cookston

"...I will answer him and care for him..."
—Hosea 14:8

Grand Traverse
Lighthouse
"Cats Head
Point"
1851

near Northport,
Michigan

Living Hope

The foundations of our Christian faith are built on trust in the God revealed by Jesus Christ and God's promise contained in His holy word. Our hope of eternal life with God, after physical death, is based on our belief in Jesus' resurrection and in the trustworthiness of His promise recorded in John 14:1-3.

The hymn writer William G. Schell poses a question that each of us, at some time in our own faith journey, will ask: *Have we any hope within us of a life beyond the grave, in the fair and vernal lands? Do we know that, when our earthly house by death shall be dissolved, We've a house not made with hands?* It is at those times of unwelcomed and unexpected or premature death that our Christian faith is most tested. All of us have known individuals (family members, friends, classmates, colleagues, acquaintances) who have died before their time. From our human perspective, it is hard for us to understand or to accept the untimely death of a child, youth or relatively young adult. Eventually, we come to the realization that the quality and influence for good of one's life is far more important than the length of a lifetime. We recognize that deceased persons' legacies of love, relationships, influence, Christian faith, and service to humankind will live on, after their death, in the memories of a multitude of friends and loved ones.

If we have received that living hope through the new birth, we can join with the hymn writer in answering the earlier question:

Blessed hope we have within us is an anchor to the soul, It is both steadfast and sure; It is founded on the promises of Father's written word, And 'twill evermore endure. If we truly believe in life after life, we can indeed rejoice in any soul's ultimate journey to be with Christ, the Light of the world, for all eternity!

David L. Coolidge

House of Light

Each December Jews around the world celebrate Hanukkah. This holiday remembers the time that the temple was rededicated after it was violated in a time of persecution a hundred and sixty years before Jesus' birth.

During the eight days of Hanukkah, a menorah (candelabra) of eight candles is lit in homes and synagogues. A legend has it that lamps which had enough oil for one day stayed lit during the eight days of the rededication.

In 1993, Billings, Montana, was the scene of several ugly attacks on its small Jewish community. As Hanukkah approached that year, Jews wondered if they dared to light their menorahs in their homes, identifying and inviting further violence.

After a cinder block was thrown through Isaac's window, destroying his menorah, the news spread rapidly across the city. Margaret McDonald, a member of First Congregational Church, read the news account and remembered how the Danish citizens during World War II wore yellow stars in solidarity with Jewish neighbors who were forced to wear yellow stars. She persuaded families in the congregation to hang menorahs in their windows as a demonstration of solidarity with their persecuted neighbors. She warned them that there were risks. Indeed, rocks were thrown and some homes were vandalized. That was enough to rouse many more in the Billings community to follow the church's example. Overnight, 10,000 menorahs were lit and hung in windows all over the city. The terror stopped.

People of faith in every age have been given the opportunity to light candles rather than curse the darkness. As long as there is hate and violence in the world there will be the challenge to face risks in working for peace, justice and righteousness, to be houses of light.

Light has come into our world and the darkness has never been able to extinguish it.

Kenneth E. Crouch

"But you are a chosen people, a royal priesthood, a holy nation, a people belonging to God, that you may declare the praises of him who called you out of darkness into his wonderful light."
—I Peter 2:9

Holland Harbor
Lighthouse
"Big Red"
1936

Holland,
Michigan

Just a Small Glimmer

I have never been trapped in a cave-in of mine shaft or earthquake, but I have observed people who were. The Mexico City earthquake on September 19, 1985, trapped thousands of persons. As I stood on a street and waited breathlessly with hundreds of others, the rescuers were listening for sounds of life beneath the massive rubble of buildings that had collapsed. Was there hope for the loved ones that were trapped? Many miraculous stories were to be told of survivors as well as the sad reality of crushing debris on frail bodies.

Hope for those in danger or despair is often ignited by just a small glimmer of light. If those who were trapped could see some light, natural or artificial, they knew rescue was possible. In our life experiences, we have many times of crisis which feel as if they are of earthquake proportions. Is there a way to find a ray of hope?

People of faith in God have an eternal light that spans the centuries and space to provide just a glimmer in our times of despair and distress. As I have stood with hundreds of mourners over my lifetime, the light in their heart and soul is everlasting. God has provided that light through His Son so that we can have hope about today and tomorrow. Just a glimmer will call forth renewed hope in most of us.

Hope for each one of us in life is absolutely essential. The greatest hope for life is the light of Jesus Christ. We will not have to walk in darkness, stumble through life, or be destroyed by life's storms if we know the light that Jesus Christ offers. One of our heritage hymns says, *My hope is built on nothing less than Jesus' blood and righteousness.* The person of faith that integrates that thought into daily life will be himself or herself a beacon of light and hope for others to follow. Follow the light and receive hope.

Ronald V. Duncan

"...I am the light of the world..."
—John 8:12

Little Sable
Point Light
1874

near
Pentwater,
Michigan

Rescued Hope

Lighthouses symbolize light and hope. As I write this, our community is rebounding from one of the worst tragedies ever in this small town—the wreckage of a school bus carrying forty-six children. An elderly lady ran a stop sign hitting the bus at the rear wheels, sending the bus reeling with no brakes. It turned over and stopped against a tree. Children were tossed like rag dolls trying in vain to brace themselves.

In minutes, the air of the usually quiet community was filled with horrifying sounds of tragedy. Fire trucks, ambulances, rescue vehicles could be heard everywhere— a continuous siren! Everyone knew something bad had happened. Three *Lifeline* helicopters, firemen, paramedics, nurses, policemen, crisis counselors, teachers, forty-one rescue units, a total of a hundred and fifteen workers converged on the scene. Fear stricken and tearful parents rushed to the scene, not knowing what they would find. It was terrifying! Injuries consisted of broken limbs, collar bones, and facial cuts, but no one was killed. The community thanked God, realizing it could have been worse.

"Be joyful in hope, patient in affliction, faithful in prayer. Share with God's people who are in need. Practice hospitality."
—Romans 12:12-13

Lighthouses symbolize protection, designed to steer away from trouble. What happens when you wreck? The lighthouse is there, it's working, and perhaps you were not watching—Bang! Is there hope after the wreck? It may be a marriage, job, dream, ministry, or your physical body! It could be a literal wreck like the one my community just experienced.

I believe there is still hope after a "wreck!" God is in the rescue business! He provides the lighthouse to warn us, then provides a rescue squad to redeem those who fail to heed the warning.

Be encouraged. If God can rescue a bus load of kids and bring hope out of chaos, He'll be there for you. Thank God for the lighthouse! Thank Him for His ability to rescue those whose lives will wreck regardless.

Ludington North Pierhead Light 1924

Ludington, Michigan

Bobby W. Dunn

54

Thoughts on Hope

I have been blessed with an optimistic outlook on life. Yes, I am one of those "the glass is half-full" people. However, possessing such an attitude is not a guarantee that life's problems pass me by. No, like everyone else, I deal with the myriad of concerns our imperfect world throws at us almost daily. Divorce, economic difficulties, death and the severe illnesses of loved ones are some of the trials that have crossed my path. Throughout these experiences I have clung to the hope that things will improve, that some good will come out of the bad, or that my attitude will become more understanding and accepting. But I haven't done that alone.

I have also been blessed with an amazingly loving family, supportive friends, and a marvelously caring fellowship of believers, my church. I'll never forget the church's outreach task force paying my winter heating bill one month or the generous check from a couple in my Sunday School class, both when I was a single parent trying to make ends meet. And I have never had to question whether my family or friends would be there for me. They have helped me in ways too numerous to count.

But there is one more element that keeps hope alive for me, and that is my faith. Without my relationship with God and my belief in His Word, my hope would be empty. There have been a few rough spots in my life when I wasn't in the company of family or friends. Then it was just God and I, and He has never failed to see me through.

I thank God for the many blessings in my life.

Carole Pistole Greenwalt

"May our Lord Jesus Christ himself and God our Father, who loved us and by his grace gave us eternal encouragement and good hope, encourage your hearts and strengthen you in every good deed and word."
—II Thessalonians 2:16-17

Old Mission Point Lighthouse
1870
near
Traverse City, Michigan

It's Never Too Late for Hope

I remember well a 1995 Indiana *Pacers* basketball game. In the breathtaking ending of the May 7 game with the New York *Knickerbockers*, Reggie Miller turned the game around. Although he had missed eleven of sixteen shots in the game, he came through at the very end. With only eighteen seconds left to play, many of the New York fans were leaving for home. In fact, the *Pacer's* coach, Larry Brown, was already thinking about what his team had done wrong to lose the game. And then Miller hit a three pointer. Intercepting the inbound pass, he took the ball behind the line for another three pointer. That tied the game. Incredibly he intercepted another inbound pass and was fouled. So he went to the line with 7.5 seconds to go in the game. He again scored with two free throws. In just 8.9 seconds on the clock the score changed from 105-99 *Knicks* to 107-105 *Pacers*.

"For I know the plans I have for you, declares the LORD, plans to prosper you and not harm you, plans to give you hope and a future."
—Jeremiah 29:11

We may think the game of life is lost, but I am reminded that no matter how it is, someone far greater than Reggie Miller is ready to change the outcome of the game. His name is Jesus Christ. Onlookers may figure that we are a lost cause. They may be leaving the stands, so to speak. Others may be using the time to figure out what went wrong with us. But the good news is that God has not left the arena. God isn't sitting on the sidelines trying to figure out what went wrong. God is still in the game. Regardless of how late it is, he says to us what he said to the ancient people of Israel whose game had gone very poorly, *"For surely I know the plans I have for you...plans for your welfare and not for harm, to give you a future with hope."* Regardless of how late it is, God is still on the playing field of our lives. He hasn't given up, and because of that, neither should we.

Point Betsie
Lighthouse
1858

near Frankfort,
Michigan

Gilbert W. Stafford

A Beacon for Darling

One might have considered her hopeless, not worth the time. Darling was a fourteen year old girl from a broken home, living with her mother, and she was very violent. The rage within her was so strong that she could not control it when dealing with others.

Darling came to our small, urban, D.C. church, to visit the Saturday night youth ministry called *Peacemakers*. She presented herself as feisty and abrasive. Yet, underneath her exterior, she was sensitive and warm-hearted.

Peacemakers was a different experience for Darling. The urban kids involved in this ministry were caring. Mack and Darlene, the leaders, treated her like their daughter. They began to tell her about the love of Jesus, God's son. And they validated that message in the way they cared for her. Quickly, Darling accepted the grace of Jesus and began a new life. It was a great celebration one Sunday morning, to baptize her as a follower of Christ, with the help of Mack.

They taught her the importance of prayer, discipline and faith. It was not long before her grades moved to passing. I remember when she was eventually moved back into the general program at her high school, which was a great accomplishment.

Today, Darling is a favorite teen at our church. Her warm character charms many. Her sensitivity toward God is very moving. God's light now helps and guides her in her daily living, through the dark nights of difficulty.

It is amazing to see God turn darkness into light through willing witnesses. Mack and Darlene are beacons of the light of Christ that shine on a host of urban youth. Their incredible love for the kids and their desire to see each one know Jesus, the Light, has brought change in what many might have called hopeless situations. They have taught me to never underestimate the transforming power of light in darkness, even from the smallest beacon.

William E. Ferguson

"There came a man who was sent from God; his name was John. He came as a witness to testify concerning that light, so that through him all men might believe. He himself was not the light; he came only as a witness to the light. The true light that gives light to every man was coming into the world."
—John 1:6-9

Nauset
Lighthouse
1873

near Eastham,
Cape Cod,
Massachusetts

Wayfinding

Little pieces
here and there
appear
tiny shells
pebbles washing up
sea glass
coming in on waves
to the sand.

A little piece
polished gem of beauty rare
discovered scavenged
a word given
on a Sunday
to the weary-eyed searcher
seeking direction
treasure
wayfinding.

Wayfinding
the revealed/revealing element
the word itself
a magnetic needle
upon the water
turning stilling
guiding.

Wayfinding
an echoing conch
a touchstone
a sliver of the blue mirror
catching light.

Wayfinding
Art Word Song Dance

Wayfinding...

Christie Smith Stephens

*"I meditate on
your precepts,
and consider
your ways."*
—Psalm 110:15

Nobska Point
Lighthouse
1876

Woods Hole,
Cape Cod,
Massachusetts

Hope Eternal

"We can do no more for her," Dr. Farley said to me concerning my wife that February afternoon, 1975. It seemed so hopeless, but I assured him that she was ready. He replied, "It's so much easier when they are at peace." Pat was at peace, filled with hope because *"having been justified by his grace, we might become heirs having the hope of eternal life."* —Titus 3:7 Christians have hope even in the face of death.

One of the greatest tragedies in life is to lose all hope. In the retirement community in which I live, there are some residents for whom life seems hopeless. To those the psalmist cries out, *"Why are you downcast, O my soul? Why so disturbed within me? Put your hope in God..."* —Psalm 42:11 God is the object of our hope; He is also the giver of hope and comfort.

Clifton Taulbert, in *Habits of the Heart* writes, "Hope, immeasurably valuable, cannot be purchased, bartered, or borrowed—it can only be shared and nurtured heart to heart." Our joy as Christians is to impart hope to others "heart to heart."

Hope is also a verb. Elizabeth Goodge in *A City of Bells*, recounts Hugh Anthony's going with his sister to see the dentist. After his grandfather rang the doorbell to the office, an awkward moment of silence followed. "Sister Henrietta suggested, 'perhaps he's gone out.' 'Perhaps he's dead,' Hugh suddenly hoped." His may have been just wishful thinking, but we all can recall, when in similar or worse circumstances, we have hoped certain events would be postponed forever. Or we have hoped for the coming of something too-good-to-be-true.

The world is in need of hope. But as Clifton Taulbert has reminded us, "The world must never forget how hope looks, acts, and feels or the obligation each individual has to practice it, share it, and pass it along."

Arthur F. Fleser

"Why are you downcast, O my soul? Why so disturbed within me? Put your hope in God, for I will yet praise him, my Savior and my God." —Psalm 42:11

Grand Haven South Pierhead Entrance *1922*

Grand Haven South Pierhead Inner *1905*

Grand Haven, Michigan

Anchored Hope

I moved to Florida to start my life over. The whole thing didn't happen like I had planned it. Divorce was something that happened to everybody else. It happened to the people I'd counseled with through twenty years of pastoral ministry. Somehow, I saw the people on the other side of the desk struggling with those types of problems as somewhat different from me.

I lived on the west coast for a lot of years. One time I lived in a little town on the Oregon coast. Reedsport, boasted a very old and quaint little lighthouse of its own. I've always been attracted to the water and to nautical symbols, lighthouses, sails, anchors and marine life.

These last several years I've suffered a kind of death and rebirth which has taken me to a new level in my understanding of this mysterious thing which we call grace. I have carried around this little stone with the word hope engraved in it. The stone now sits in a little meditation fountain in the foyer to my office.

God has brought people and resources into my life that have helped me navigate, survive and at times even flourish as I've traveled to this oasis of mine on the Gulf coast of Florida. I can almost see another lighthouse standing on the beach across the street from my new home. I don't know if I believe in the concept of *karma* but it's clear to me that through the mercy of God, we are constantly given new opportunities to "get things right" and to begin again.

"We have this hope as an anchor for the soul." One time I delivered a sermon on this text and an Anderson University sculptor fashioned a beautiful bronze piece of art based on the homily as a gift to me. It is one of my most prized possessions.

Kenneth L. Gill

"We have this hope as an anchor for the soul..."
—Hebrews 6:19

Heceta Head
Lighthouse
1894

near
Florence, Oregon

Child of Hope and Light

It was three o'clock in the morning and I had only been in bed for a couple of hours. I was exhausted from making trips to the hospital where my wife was a patient in the OB/GYN Intensive Care Unit and our home about an hour away. My wife had been hospitalized in the twenty-fifth week of her pregnancy five days earlier. I had been busy organizing care for our two year old son, spending time at the hospital with my wife, and arranging coverage for the hospice where I serve as a pastoral counselor.

It took me a moment to realize the phone was ringing. I remembered thinking that it is usually not good when the phone rings in the middle of the night. My wife was on the other end of the line. Her voice sounded soft and kind of groggy...she told me to come back to the hospital right away because the doctors needed to go in and take the baby very soon. As I drove to the hospital I prayed for mercy and grace for my wife and unborn baby. I was in a state of shock.

It all happened very quickly, walking to the operating room, signing papers, meeting several different kinds of doctors, being told where to sit. I was holding my wife's hand when the doctor wrapped up our baby and the nurse took the baby away. I asked if anyone noticed if it was a boy or girl and of the five doctors and four nurses present, no one noticed. It all happened very fast. Our son, as it turned out, was moved to a Neo-natal Intensive Care Unit in a hospital next door. After my wife was stabilized and resting I went to see our son. I had only seen his face for a moment before they moved him.

I had never seen a premature baby before. Our son weighed one pound and five ounces and was hooked up

Owl's Head
Light Station
1826

near
Rockland, Maine

Continued on page 70

68

Lighthouse in
Pendleton Park
1928

Pendleton,
Indiana

to machines to help him breathe, to keep him warm, and every kind of monitor you can imagine. I remembered that one of the doctors had said that infants born this early have about a fifty percent chance of making it through the first week. He looked so small and powerless that I thought fifty percent seemed extremely optimistic. I am a person of faith, but I certainly had difficulty holding on to hope.

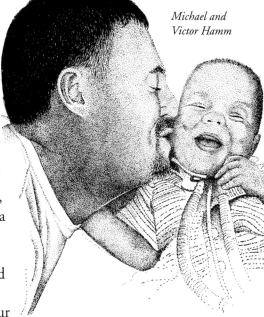

*Michael and
Victor Hamm*

Then I received a visitor. A man of deep spiritual faith, a wounded healer, a friend and mentor, came to visit. He told me that he had a dream about our son. Speaking to our son, he said, "I have seen you in a dream, little man, and I know you are a child of God." His gentle voice brought calm into the room. He said to me, "When I see him, I do not see a tiny little baby...I see an extremely powerful spirit whom God has blessed. His spirit shines brightly."

I learned to see our son in a new light that day. My friend encouraged me to have hope and faith. His example and witness were contagious. Medically, it was difficult to be hopeful. Spiritually, the Holy Spirit provided the hope we needed. As I write this, we are preparing to celebrate Victor's first birthday. He is a child of hope and light.

Michael A.V. Hamm

Source of Hope

As a pastor, I have encountered many hurting and troubled people. Some situations seemed hopeless and I struggled for ways to help. Occasionally I have asked, "How can you be so optimistic, given your circumstances?" And I often inquired of my own sources of hope for them. Did I really trust God?

Christian believers have a source of hope that goes beyond surroundings, or scientific evidence, or enthusiasm, or wishful thinking. That source, like a lighthouse on a rocky shore, is none other than our Triune God who promises never to forsake us. We can choose to place our hope in the Lord of the universe!

Life often tests our trust. In January, 1992, I was diagnosed with bladder cancer. Various treatment options gave me thirty percent, fifty percent, and seventy percent chances of living another five years. One day I went into Miller Chapel at Anderson University to spend some time in prayer. I had been bombarded with information, probabilities and options. I needed a word from God.

The beautiful stained glass window depicts Jesus with outstretched arms. As I sat in silence, I listened with hope. What I got was the simple yet profound word: I will be with you...I did not ask for a miracle of physical healing. I didn't need to. That my Lord would be with me made everything else all right. I had peace.

So, I continue to live in hope. I am accompanied on my journey. I have seen the Light and no darkness can extinguish it!

Dwight L. Grubbs

"...he will never leave you nor forsake you."
—Deuteronomy 31:0

"I will not leave you..."
—John 14:18

"...I am with you always..."
—Matthew 28:20

Big Sable
Point Lighthouse
1900

near
Ludington,
Michigan

A Beacon in a Storm

Life is what happens while you're planning other things. The reality of that truism smacked my wife, Joyce, and me squarely in the face the summer of 1999. Her doctor was concerned about a lump in the breast. Biopsy confirmed our worst fears...cancer. Surgery and chemotherapy took its usual terrible physical and emotional toll. We cried, prayed, threw some pity parties and a couple of books. But after several months the worst was over, and life began settling into a comfortable routine again. We look back with gratitude that it's over, and that together we survived a frightening experience. Some fear remains. Fighting cancer is a battle won one day at a time. It's never completely won, however, because the disease can reappear. Still, we purposefully talk about having had cancer, never using the present tense.

It's clear that hope brought us through. Not head-in-the-sand hoping for the best in spite of the truth. Long ago we laid the foundation of our lives upon hope in the Lord Jesus. Through the years His grace has blessed and nurtured that youthful affirmation of trust. *My hope is built on nothing less than Jesus' blood and righteousness. On Christ, the solid rock, I stand, all other ground is sinking sand,* proclaims the hymn.

Like a beacon in a storm, this hope has given Joyce and me direction through the worst experience of our thirty-two years together. God felt our heartache and sent reassurance in the form of praying family and friends. We felt His comforting presence in the face of fear. And we're reminded that the reward for trusting is paradise. How many times have we heard the message? Now, I understand. Now, I believe.

Leslie H. Mosier

"*Cast all your anxiety on him because he cares for you.*"
—I Peter 5:7

Rock of Ages
Lighthouse
1908

Isle Royale,
Michigan

All I Have Needed

My cousin, Launa, Mama's oldest brother's third daughter, and I were talking about her daddy, Walter, and my mama, Pearl. We were talking about how they had lived and how they had died.

I told her I am sure that it was Walter who came for his little sister, Pearl. Walter who stood there on the other side of Jordan reaching out his hand for hers when she passed through the waters in January of 1995. I am sure because it was his name she called out in the dying days.

We both remembered vividly Walter's home-going in 1986, and we remember that he left us with a grin on his face. His wife, Launa's mother, my Aunt Mildred said, "It's hard to grieve when he's got a grin on his face. It's hard to grieve when he's got a grin on his face."

Launa told me that before Walter died Miss Mildred, as we sometimes affectionately call her, was always fearful when he would go anywhere and she'd be home alone, but since his death she hasn't been afraid about much of anything. Could be that he is with her all the time now.

She lives out in the country in a little community known as Harmony Hill directly across the highway from the Harmony Hill Church of God. There is a barn out back of the house and it has a light on it. When Walter, her husband of fifty-something years, died that light went out. Aunt Mildred, as usual, spoke to God about the situation. She said matter of factly, "Now, God, You know I need that light."

And the light came back on and stayed on for years...
And the light came back on and stayed on for years...

Christie Smith Stephens

"...I am the light of the world. Whoever follows me will never walk in darkness, but will have the light of life."
—John 8:12

"Now faith is being sure of what we hope for and certain of what we do not see."
—Hebrews 11:1

Baileys Harbor
Front & Rear
Range Lights
1870

Baileys Harbor,
Wisconsin

76

Beacons of Light — Little Girl Faces

Beacons of light, along the way. Morning sunshine on little faces—in all kinds of places. "Papa, Nana, where is God?" "Oh, Charis, Sarah, Hannah, Rachel and Gabrielle, He is everywhere! And most of all in you, little girl faces, full of God's graces."

Playing, singing, dreaming, squealing, and snuggling. Oh the glory, the thrill of a new day and little girl faces!

Beacons of light, they lead us.

Meadows of mountain iris, purples and blues on little girl faces. Gently, lovingly, they touch them, they hold them, they smell them—they sit and lie down in them. They look at them and the big blue sky away up high. Real, amazing, eternal—pure joy.

Beacons of light, they teach us.

"The Lord is my light and my salvation—whom shall I fear?..."
—Psalm 27:1

Cheboygan
Crib Light
1910

Cheboygan,
Michigan

Wading and playing, in crystal clear waters.
Baptizing dollies in the creek. They speak, so meek,
"In Jesus' name."

Water splashing, beacons of light...

Curled up in our laps, heads on our breasts,
"Tell us a story." They listen, they pat us,
comfort us—trust us. They rest.

Beacons of light, they show us how to love,
how to live best.

Continued on page 80

When the sun is setting, "Daddy, Daddy, let's climb a
mountain!" Hands holding hands, running up the
hillside. Wind in their faces—angels' wings lift them,
carry them far—carry them far.

Beacons of hope, smiling little faces.

Sitting by the crackling fire, hot dogs, marshmallows and
sparklers—light on sticky sweet faces. Hand in hand,
little fingers touching mine—counting one, two, three,
four, five, "Mine are just like yours!"

God, help us, beacon of light. Shine in us!

Ending of the day, little hands still—Heads bowed,
hushed sweet songs, eyes closed and soft whispers.
"Dear God, I love you, dear God, thank you."

Beacons of light, they worship.

Evening shadows fall. Pure love,
God's love leading—leading us on.

Beacons of light, leading us on...

*Reflections from my journal about granddaughters on
Colorado family vacation—July, 1999*

Sylvia Kennedy Grubbs

Fort Gratiot
Light
1861

Port Huron,
Michigan

Hope — Strong, Sure, Steadfast

The lighthouse at Ponce de Leon Inlet, just south of Daytona Beach, Florida, guided mariners past treacherous shoals at the edge of the Atlantic from 1887 to 1970. This graceful brick tower reaches 175 feet into the sky and its piercing light beams far out to sea. It is a favorite of ours because of its graceful strength and its stories past, but especially because of the special message of hope it brings.

While hope takes a justified place alongside faith and love in I Corinthians 13, this virtue is so often practiced in a weak and spasmodic way. It sometimes shows up simply as a passing fancy or a half-hearted grasping at straws. A lighthouse like the one at Ponce Inlet, however, is a symbol that shows what real hope can be.

Lighthouses are built as towers of hope. The faith is there that the light will be seen, the warning bells and horns heard to help wandering mariners avoid danger and find safety. Lighthouses are not guarantees of safety, but they are strong signs of hope that they will alert needy persons of danger, that they will guide them to safety.

The lighthouse at Ponce Inlet speaks to us about hope with its firm foundation, steadfast serenity, and a light that pierces darkness and distance. Climbing to the top of Ponce Lighthouse offers us a perspective on the whole area. We can find the lay of the land, come to understand how things really are from this tower. It has also served as an encouragement. We can dare to find our way out into the waves, knowing that the lighthouse is there to guide and to help us on our return. It backs us in being judicious risk takers.

Standing firm and sure, tall and graceful, the lighthouse offers a message larger than simply safety to nearby seafarers.

Arlene and Kenneth Hall

"For in this hope we were saved...But if we hope for what we do not yet have, we wait for it patiently."
—Romans 8:24-25

Ponce de Leon Inlet Lighthouse
1887

Ponce Inlet, Florida

Found Hope

Barbara Glatzell was ten when both mother and father died. She was "farmed out" to an aunt who immediately took her out of school and put her to work six days a week, ten hours a day, selling pickles, sauerkraut, and olives in a farmer's market. In addition to near slave conditions, Barbara was subjected to ridicule and degradation in the home. The child's sheer loneliness, the loss of both parents and the inhuman treatment ground Barbara down. No friends and the light of hope was dimming.

The years dragged by for her. Life got more gloomy each day. In fact hope was almost gone when she found the church and gave her life to Christ. A brand new corner of bright hope was turned and although twenty-eight, still single and living a harsh life, Barbara made a decision. She'd go to college. With her fifth grade education and the little cash she'd saved from her hard work, off she went to the Anderson Bible Training School in Indiana.

More hard work, but now life was good, friends became plentiful. At thirty-three, still single, she was ordained to full time Christian ministry, selected as associate pastor of a thriving church and began leading a large band of followers in Christian education and evangelism. The years that followed were filled with hundreds upon hundreds of opportunities to serve people, lead training sessions and be a sweet counselor to dozens and dozens of unmarried women. "God's unclaimed gems," she called them.

Nearly sixty years later she laid down the mantle after a lifetime of humble, dedicated service, still saying, "Without my hope in Christ, I'd still be selling pickles in that market."

Daniel C. Harman

"I pray also that the eyes of your heart may be enlighened in order that you may know the hope to which he called you, the riches of his glorious inheritance in the saints, and his incomparably great power for us who believe..."
—Ephesians 1:18-19

Chatham
Lighthouse
1877

Chatham,
Cape Cod,
Massachusetts

The Light

On Christmas Eve we consider "The Light." From Isaiah 9:2—

> *"The people who walked in darkness have*
> *seen a great light;*
> *those who lived in a land of deep darkness—*
> *on them light has shined."*

Perhaps we can remember once again, our life is not a matter of what we do, what we have, who we know, or where we've been. Our life in Christ is a matter of the light—the light by which we are guided; the light from which we are warmed, the light from which we are nourished and resourced.

Jesus said, *"I am the light that has come into the world. No one who has faith in me will stay in the dark."*
—John 12:45-46

Jesus also said to us, *"Walk in the light. Have faith in the light, and you will be children of light."*
—John 12:35-36

Children raise their small index fingers in the air and enthusiastically sing, *This little light mine, I'm going to let it shine.* The popular lyrics sometimes used in a religious context ring out *You Light Up My Life.*

And Paul reminds us in Ephesians, *"Now you are people of the light because you belong to the Lord. So act like people of the light and make your light shine."*
—Ephesians 5:8

In this sacred time of memory, reflection and commitment may the light that is the Christ illuminate our hearts. For the one who was promised so long ago has come, and this revelation of God, this gift of God is *our* light to claim, and is the light in which we walk.

Christmas Eve, 1997
Anita Smith Womack

"The people walking in darkness have seen a great light; on those living in the land of the shadow of death a light has dawned."
—Isaiah 9:2

Sanibel Island
Lighthouse
1884

Sanibel, Florida

Ashtabula Memories

Prospects of a warm summer afternoon were all it would take for three young boys from Boy Scout Troop 12 at the Episcopal Church of Ashtabula, Ohio, to meet in front of the church at Main Street Park to go fishing and swimming at Lake Shore Park. Fishing and swimming in Lake Erie were popular summer pastimes.

There were two ways to get to the park, a four-mile bike ride. One, the quickest and most direct, was to take State Road. The other, farther, but more interesting, wound its way through Ashtabula Harbor. Leaving early in the morning, fishing and swimming gear in tow, we usually would choose the State Road route. Our hope would be that we would get there before the early morning fog lifted from the lake, to hear the deep foghorn of the Ashtabula Lighthouse, alerting the big iron ore laden ships of their closeness to the harbor. Occasionally we would glimpse the powerful beacon swinging its way back and forth across the fog-covered lake.

Returning home, we would take the longer route through the harbor. The hope would be that we would arrive at the giant lift bridge in time to watch it lower its massive concrete weight, raising the bridge to allow the huge ore boats to pass and move slowly into the shipyards for repair.

Small but powerful tugboats slowly moved the giant ships through the narrow passages and shallow waters. Later they would tug them back out into Lake Erie to continue their assignments. More than one sermon illustration came from those boyhood memories.

Now I read about the docking of the spaceship *Endeavor* at the International Space Station and wonder, "Do they have 'tugboats'?"

Sherrill D. Hayes

"He has made everything beautiful in its time..."
—Ecclesiastes 3:11

Ashtabula
Harbor
Lighthouse
1905

Ashtabula, Ohio

When Every Child

When every child
      is a child of love born free
            in a justice world,

When every child
      is a child of hope whose dreams
            like wings unfurl,

When every child
      is a child of peace in a home
            where violence is no more,

When every child
      is a child of joy whose songs
            like angels soar,

When every child
      is a child of light whose eyes
            shine in the night so sweet,

When every child
      is the child the church lifts up
            then the mission will be complete.

When every child...
      When every child...
            When every child...

          Christie Smith Stephens

South Haven
South Pierhead
Light
1903

South Haven,
Michigan

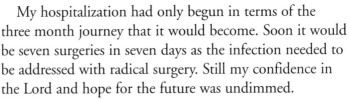

He Shaved My Arm! There Is Hope!!!

"Therefore my heart is glad and my tongue rejoices; my body also will live in hope,..."
—Acts 2:26

My hospitalization had only begun in terms of the three month journey that it would become. Soon it would be seven surgeries in seven days as the infection needed to be addressed with radical surgery. Still my confidence in the Lord and hope for the future was undimmed.

Then, after a bandage from the amputation was changed I started to bleed. At first unnoticed this soon became cause for alarm. The "code" went out, and soon I was attended by multiple doctors. One soon pronounced my blood pressure and said "We're losing him." Not afraid to die, but certainly anxious, I rehearsed the "good-byes" I would have shared if my family had been present. And I waited, wondering what the end would be like.

The attending resident doctor arrived and determined I needed another intravenous feed to get my fluid levels elevated. And then it happened. He shaved my arm. In my mind I knew he did not want it to hurt when the tape was later removed—and therefore it was obvious to me, there was hope.

Later I was asked by several of those attending, what had happened to me that changed my sense of what was happening. I told them— "He shaved my arm." What to them was standard medical practice, was to me a sign of hope.

On the day of Pentecost, Peter quoted from David in Psalm 16: *"Therefore my heart is glad and my tongue rejoices; my body also will live in hope,..."* —Acts 2:26

My heart was gladdened as he shaved my arm, and still today my body lives in hope.

How routine an act inspires hope.

John A. Howard

Manistee North
Pierhead Light
1927

Manistee,
Michigan

Nantucket

"There is a time for everything, and a season for every activity under heaven: a time to be born and a time to die, a time to plant and a time to uproot, a time to kill and a time to heal, a time to tear down and a time to build, a time to weep and a time to laugh, a time to mourn and a time to dance, a time to scatter stones and a time to gather them, a time to embrace and a time to refrain, a time to search and a time to give up, a time to keep and a time to throw away, a time to tear and a time to mend, a time to be silent and a time to speak, a time to love and a time to hate, a time for war and a time for peace.
—Ecclesiastes 3:1-8

Brant Point
Lighthouse
1901

Nantucket,
Massachusetts

The heaviness of the Indiana humidity hits my face like dead reality. I am home. Time to think about the laundry, my hair appointment on Tuesday, my fall classes, picking up Mowgli, the kids' library books. But for a while, I was dreaming a thick, fog-laden dream, and I was walking up India Street in a fleece sweatshirt, my hair pulled back into a ponytail, telling Will and Jesse that just ahead is the wharf where, tied to wooden and iron posts, the paint-chipped dinghies rest, still and silent. "I came here as a girl," I say. Somewhere the horn of the Nantucket ferry sounds its warning.

Will, in his favorite "Nantucket Red" sweater, and Jesse, in gray sweats, pull at my hands, eyes wide, asking questions—Will the philosophical one, phrasing posers like, "How old were you when you were here?" and "Why do we have to be careful on the dunes?" and "Did whales really smash boats into pieces like in those pictures at the Whaling Museum?" —Jesse, speaking in monosyllabic punches, like, "Dog," "Er's Mamaw?" and "Deece, hand!"

The images are perfect and picturesque and ancient, even now with my own small children so centrally featured. I look at the paintings in Old South Wharf Galleries portraying early Nantucket life, children in bloomers and straw hats whose parents used whale blubber for lamp oil and I think that in that setting those children could be any children, could be my children.

The man on the video tour of Nantucket explained why the island has remained so quaint. It seems that after the world began using petroleum instead of whale oil for heat and light there was little need for the island, her resources, and her trade. So having never gone through any sort of industrial revolution, the island was frozen in time for years until tourists, weary of their busy, stressful lives on the continent, rediscovered her. And that

Continued on page 96

explains it, the pull Nantucket has on all of us. It comes like a cast iron anchor, not from something fabricated to look real like *Disneyland*, but from a literal "otherworldliness," from a time when the pleasures of life were simple and work was hard, even perilous and fatal, from a land that built character with salt into the wrinkled faces of its people and wore their skin as gray as the shingles on Jed Coffin's old house, from cobblestone streets where horses once clip-clopped past the bricked Three Sisters who still stand as a testimony to perseverance, from the stalwart Brandt Point Lighthouse built in 1746 to illuminate the way for lost sailors, from the intricate pieces of scrimshaw in the Whaling Museum made on long voyages by sailors who had too much time to think—all so intriguing to us and luring, beckoning as Ahab did strapped to the great, white Moby Dick.

We lose perspective until we are islanders again. "No man is an island," John Donne said, but I say every man is an island connected only to sky, and our souls are sick until we separate them again from continents that latch onto us so tightly they obscure our original form. We step off the ferry barnacled and enervated and leave smooth and stripped of parasites.

On our last night on Dionis, I felt it, watching the boys smear themselves with dust and sand, jump and scoot down the dunes, hunt for sea treasures, and eat coal-roasted hot dogs that "never tasted so good."

In my mind's eye, I look around at our dear sea mates: Peggy, alone here again without Bob; Joy, so full of vigor and intellect and worry; Mac, thankful and giddy; Dad and Fred, full of good humor; Mom soaking in her element; Amy, Steven, Shana, and Mark, guards down, children again; Danny and Vonnie, proud of their accomplishments; Benjy, lost in thought, fishing; Lois and little Lee, enchanted, captivated; Barry, relaxed, cuddling the children. And I see us all, separate entities communing with sky, stripped of make-up and hair spray and modesty and pretentiousness.

We are the people in the paintings displayed in galleries on the Old South Wharf. We are in bloomers and straw hats on holiday searching for shells. We are lonely, pacing the creaky floors of widow's walks. We are worn from perilous voyages. We are children. We have too much time to think. We are the Three Sisters, strong and ancient. We are worn gray as cedar shingles. We have been here before. The anchor that holds us is heavy.

Suzanne Gaither Jennings

Presque Isle Lighthouse *1873*
Presque Isle, Pennsylvania

A Tiny Light in the Darkness

Everyone understands "light" and "dark." We take "lightness" and "darkness" for granted. For me, at least, I never really gave much consideration to the real meanings of those words—it was simply "light" or "dark" or shades in between.

However, one summer we were traveling with a group of young people from California to Louisville, Kentucky, to attend a youth convention. We decided to go via Carlsbad Caverns in New Mexico and to spend a day exploring in the caverns. We were assigned a ranger-guide who gave us an explanation of how the caverns were formed. And then we set out on our journey!

After we had walked quite some distance into the caverns admiring the stalactites and stalagmites, the many other rock formations, and the enormous caves, we were asked, "Have you ever been in total darkness? Can you imagine what it must be like to be in absolute, total darkness?"

The guide told us to remain exactly where we were—not to move! The lights were turned off! We were in total darkness! Really, in this world, we are seldom in total darkness. But that day we were—there was no light anywhere! We could not see a bit of light at a cave opening, no light above and none in front of us or at our feet. I remember moving my hand in front of my face but I could detect nothing. It was total darkness!

After allowing us to ponder the darkness a few moments, our guide turned on a tiny flashlight—it was tiny but in the darkness it was a great light! We could see our guide, our friends, and the surroundings. How thankful I am for light! There is a scripture in which I am reminded again and again to be thankful for *"Jesus, the light of the world."* —John 8:12

Betty Jo Hyman Johnson

"...the LORD turns my darkness into light."
—II Samuel 22:29

Umpqua River Lighthouse
1804

near
Winchester Bay,
Oregon

Hope

goes beyond purpose and direction to expectancy
longs, desires, cherishes, anticipates
sees beneath surfaces to deepest beauties and hidden
    loveliness
lives at the deepest foundation of life
strikes at the heart of what human means and humanity
    at its best
looks forward face toward the sun
sleeps through the storm
believes in God's kingdom now

    says it will not always be thus
    says it will get better
    says life is always darker just before dawn
    says, yes, Virginia, there is a Santa Claus
    says, in spite of this

has wings and flies
has a blind man's hands
has dancer's feet
has troubadour's song
has an actor's diaphragm
has a conductor's certainty about the score

    a bird singing in the snow on the coldest day
      of the year
    flowers in the desert

a waiting parent staring down a road
a Baby in a manger, a thoughtful Mother,
    and an anxious father
a cross and empty tomb

"Why are you downcast, O my soul,
    and why are you disquieted within me?
Hope in God; for I shall again praise him,
    my help and my God." —Psalm 42:5 NRSV

Arthur M. Kelly

"Why are you downcast, O my soul? Why so disturbed within me? Put your hope in God, for I will yet praise him, my Savior and my God..."
—Psalm 42:5-6

Yaquina Bay
Lighthouse
1871

Newport, Oregon

A Light to the Nations

"I, the LORD,
have called you
in righteousness;
I will take hold
of your hand.
I will keep you
and will make
you to be a
covenant for the
people and a
light to the
Gentiles, to open
eyes that are
blind, to free
captives from
prison and to
release from the
dungeon those
who sit in
darkness."
—Isaiah 42:6-7

It is difficult for me to look at a lighthouse or even a picture of one without thinking of the Biblical use of the word "light." More particularly for me it pertains to the Gospel as being light to the nations. There is a personal mandate for me to be the keeper of the light.

Several years ago when I was the pastor of a church of world Christians I periodically would choose from among them a person whose mission it was in life to protect the light and focus it on persons who needed to be illuminated—those in need for whatever reason. I had a potter fashion a small clay oil lamp that I presented to each individual in public worship.

In a larger sense, these persons, these keepers of the light became models for all of us. It was clear to everyone who knew them—to everyone who had been ministered to by them, that they represented the best, which we ourselves desired to be.

It is we, now, who are the "New Israel." It is we who are to be a light to the nations—keepers of the light!

Donald D. Johnson

Cape Disappointment Lighthouse 1850

near Seaview, Washington

Two Lights

The St. Joseph Light

Late at night I hear the drone of the foghorn. Even with modern radar, the ship captains need to hear its horn and see its flashing light to maneuver into the harbor.

The lighthouse is built at the mouth of the St. Joseph River where it empties into Lake Michigan. On the north pier a tall catwalk stretches to the red roofed lighthouse, and when storms and high waves crash over the piers, the Coast Guard can walk safely on it and attend to the lighthouse.

A Signal—Our lighthouse warns of stormy weather or fog-filled nights, telling the early rising fisherman to stay in bed or signaling ships running along the western coast to "stay out in deep waters where it is safe to sail."

Protection—Sailboats, fishing boats, barges, ships of all kinds, moor at the docks beyond the lighthouse in the harbor. When the wind blows out on the lake, peaceful waters wait there.

A Gathering Place—In the summer, children play in the sand near the lighthouse, building sandcastles. Fishermen line the piers, shoulder to shoulder in the fall, all the way out to the lighthouse. At sunset, families holding tightly to children, couples hand in hand, old and young, crowd past the lighthouse to get a closer look at the sun setting, sometimes cheering as it melts out of sight.

There is strength, beauty, and comfort in the St. Joe Lighthouse. Like the church, which Jesus built, it is a signal to those who might be bouncing in the waves of life or perhaps wandering in the fog of loneliness and despair. The church offers protection for people who respond. They find comfort in the Holy Spirit and strength in His word. It is a gathering place where people give encouragement, hope, and love, as they all journey together.

Dale D. Landis

"Trust in the LORD with all your heart and lean not on your own understanding; in all your ways acknowledge him, and he will make your paths straight."
—Proverbs 3:5-6

St. Joseph
North Pier
Lighthouses
Outer/Inner
1907

St. Joseph,
Michigan

West Beirut Lighthouse

"Here is my servant, whom I uphold, my chosen one in whom I delight; I will put my Spirit on him and he will bring justice to the nations."

"I, the LORD, have called you in righteousness; I will take hold of your hand. I will keep you and will make you to be a covenant for the people and a light for the Gentiles, to open eyes that are blind, to free captives from prison and to release from the dungeon those who sit in darkness."
—Isaiah 42:1,6-7

West Beirut Lighthouse "Manara"

West Beirut, Lebanon

Not far from my children's school in the heavily Muslim half of West Beirut there is a neighborhood called *Manara*, simply meaning "lighthouse." For years a *manara* has stood on the high hill of that rocky section of Beirut's coastline that juts into the Mediterranean Sea, stabbing light into the inky blackness, warning ships of danger and offering hope of safe passage.

The *manara* still stands today. Once, no doubt, it was a solitary point of light along that coastline. Today the city has grown up around the *manara*. In fact, if you didn't know it was there, you might miss it. In the bright light of day the *manara* blends into the cityscape. However, in the dark of night the light pulsates from the reflective glass within the simple tower.

As I drive along that section of road in the evenings, particularly during the days of Advent, I think about that lighthouse. I think of the message of warning and the message of hope. I think about the declaration of the prophet Isaiah.

My prayer is for the people who live in the densely populated Muslim sections of West Beirut. It is a prayer that Christ, God's *Manara*, would find acceptance in their hearts and the justice and righteousness of God would be freed from the prison house of Islam, and that the hope of Christ will shine in their dark world.

But it is not just for those who are bound by the darkness of Islam on whom the light of Christ has shined. God's *Manara* shines into the darkness or the prison houses of sin, indifference, self-righteousness, rebellion, discouragement, and loneliness. The hope of Christ continues to shine in our dark world as well.

John M. Johnson

The Sunflower

For Simon Wiesenthal
Holocaust Survivor

I read your book,
The Sunflower,
On the Possibilities
and Limits of Forgiveness.
You asked,
What would you
have done in my place?

What would I
have done in your place?
And I answer,
Just what you did
if I were having
a really good day.

Silence rather than
Spoken Forgiveness.
Silence rather than...

Silence costs so much.
A dying while living still.
Silence often a gift,
a mercy beyond pardon,
a sunflower in ice.

You gave it twice
in critical moments,
then told the story
leaving *The Question*
where it always belongs—
in the hand, heart and soul
of each human being.

I give thanks for your silence.
I give thanks for your question.
I give thanks for *Your Sunflower.*

Your silence shines in a world
that too often, too easily,
too quickly responds with
what we think we must believe,
not with what we really live.

You are light.
You are hope.

I send you bouquets of flowers
of your own choosing,
In Remembrance...
In Remembrance...

Christie Smith Stephens

Eagle Bluff Lighthouse *1868*
Pennisula State Park, Wisconsin

Higher Hope

It has been said the most difficult of human endeavors is to go to the next thing. Our propensity is to remain encumbered in the present thing. We tend to sail our ship of life on the chosen voyage of yesterday.

The beacon that takes us to the next thing is hope. Without it our desires and expectations never come together to prod us to action; our ship takes on water, embroiled in the mires of the past. With hope that is in the Father's will, we become energized to be agents of a higher hope.

> To look into the night
> and hope for the light.
> When all is dark
> and all the patterns fail,
> and the prison of the present state
> bids we acquiesce and wait
> and hide within our sinking shell,
> requires the turning of the soul
> to the ancient port,
> to the hope of the ages past.
> To the sure stronghold
> where hope in this transient state
> is put in proper scope by One
> who said, *"Not my will, but Thine be done."*

Ronald O. Hall

"Return to your fortress, O prisoners of hope; even now I announce that I will restore twice as much to you."
—Zechariah 9:12

Bass Harbor
Head Light
1858

Mount Desert
Island, Maine

Whispering Hope

His disciples huddled in fear and total despair, hearts torn by grief and empty of all hope. But God had a plan, a plan that did not allow for the extinguishing of His light for the world. Incredibly, unbelievably as Sunday dawned, hope was reborn; the world has never been the same.

In the deepest sorrows and blackest nights of our human experience, the flame of hope is often a mere flicker. The hymn, *Whispering Hope,* was loved by my mother and still speaks to us in our spiritual journeys of hope *whispering her comforting word.* When the *darkness is over...the tempest is done...*we can hope for *sunshine tomorrow, after the shower is gone.*

God does not spare us the pain, sorrows, illnesses and disasters that beset all humankind. His only promise is that He will walk with us through them, even though we may not feel His presence.

We felt a whisper of hope when genetic researchers found the defective gene that causes Huntington's Disease which has destroyed three of my sister's family. We have witnessed the terrible ravages of Alzheimer's Disease. We know premature babies, suddenly dead, can shock the human spirit into numbness and overwhelming grief but it cannot destroy the hope of life eternal. Hope may be only a whisper but it is a whisper the faithful hear. His great purpose cannot be defeated even by death and nothing can snatch us from God's loving care.

Madelyn Taylor Hartman

"Therefore, since we have been justified through faith, we have peace with God through our Lord Jesus Christ, through whom we have gained access by faith into this grace in which we now stand. And we rejoice in the hope of the glory of God."
—Romans 5:1-2

Michigan City Light
1858

Michigan City, Indiana

Portland Head Light

Hope Is Our Anchor!

The call came in the middle of the night. Marti had suffered a brain aneurysm and had been transported to a Chicago hospital for emergency treatment. But as the hours passed, the treatment was in doubt. The bleeding had caused swelling and surgery was impossible. The doctor was at a loss to know what step to take and when!

Her family gathered in the hospital chapel and joined in prayer. We prayed for her healing. We prayed for her deliverance. We prayed that the doctor would know the right action for remedy. We sought the Great Physician!

There, in the quiet of that place, we learned about hope. We wanted Marti returned to us and we stated that in our prayers. Then, we were reminded of the story of Abraham's willingness to sacrifice his son Isaac and the resulting blessing of God. So we surrendered Marti's life into the safekeeping of God and recognized that our great hope was in the wondrous sacrifice made for us at Calvary. Marti had accepted that gift and now was ready for eternal life. That great hope gave us peace.

We hoped that somehow Marti might survive and be returned to her family. But the greater hope was the reality that the substitute sacrifice had been already offered and Marti had embraced that gift. She could not lose! No matter what happened next, our hope had been strengthened by the awareness that we need not attempt to dictate the outcome.

The miracles which followed...the correct decisions at the right moment...the care and expertise of medicine...the touch of God in witness to others and on Marti's body were all evidence of God's hand and answer to our prayers. She lives and is a walking example of the power in which we trusted. We rejoice in that. But, even more, we rejoice in the knowledge that our hope goes beyond this life and that it offers the anchor for our souls, firm and secure!

David L. Lawson

"We have this hope as an anchor for the soul, firm and secure. It enters the inner sanctuary behind the curtain, where Jesus, who went before us, has entered on our behalf..."
—Hebrews 6:19

CapeNeddick
Lighthouse
"Nubble Light"
1879

near
York Beach,
Maine

Meditation on Light and Hope

Hope is said to be something without which we cannot live. This seems to be true, but what is the basis of hope? Hope is never blind, nor is it a grasping at straws. Rather, hope is founded on a basic fact that in the physical world light always penetrates darkness, not the other way around. By its very nature, light advances into darkness, not darkness into light. Wherever there is light, darkness recedes and slinks back to become shadows. It can't overcome light.

That is also the basis of hope in our world of human relationships and activities. However, the effective instrument of *light* is not a candle, match, or bulb. It is life—from the Christian understanding, it is founded on a specific life, that of Jesus Christ. Then we are called to follow Him, to join our lives to His so that, as one candle lights another, His *life light* is transferred to ours and thus through us penetrates and dispels the spiritual and moral darkness that is real and pervasive in our world today.

The challenge is that where there is no light, then darkness does indeed take over—by default. Only the presence of a *life light* can advance love and offer hope, and thus dispel the darkness. Since that first *life light* was Himself crucified and buried, we are talking serious business. It may mean the sacrifice of something important to us and in us—our *death* figuratively or even literally. But we have the promise that as He was raised to new life, so too will we.

So we must answer: will we unite with that first *life light* to become a beacon of hope that pushes back the darkness in our own world?

L. David Lewis

"In him was life, and that life was the light of men. The light shines in the darkness, but the darkness has not understood it."
—John 1:4-5

Old Mackinac Point Lighthouse
1892

Mackinaw City, Michigan

Writing by Gaslight

During my junior year in high school my family rented and was living in a small farmhouse on the outskirts of Indianapolis. The house was situated approximately a quarter of a mile from what was then known as the Rock Island Refinery.

Early in the new year of 1961 a fierce winter storm struck on a Saturday night. The wind blew with great strength and snow fell for many hours. On Sunday morning the snow on our little country road had drifted four to five feet high.

Sometime in the evening hours our power went out. My mother and I decided we'd be better off going to bed and to sleep to wait out the storm. My father was hard at work writing the dissertation for his Doctor of Philosophy degree. He feared that his thoughts would evaporate with the sunrise if he didn't keep writing. He sought a spot to write that was lighted almost like daylight by the powerful flame at the refinery.

In the calm morning light he was all smiles, pleased that his words were safely recorded and his goal still in sight.

In your life experiences may you allow the powerful light of Christ to guide you in your accomplishment of the goals He has set before you.

Avis Kleis Liverett

"For God, who said, 'Let light shine out of the darkness,' made his light shine in our hearts to give us the light of the knowledge of the glory of God in the face of Christ."
—II Corinthians 4:6

Cape Elizabeth Lighthouse
"Two Lights"
1874

Cape Elizabeth, Maine

Two Lights

118

Two Lights

A Poem Celebrating the Marriage of
Kathleen Mary McCormick and
Mark David Liverett
You are the Light of the World.

You stand grounded
on old stone rocks
marked by fallen trees
high above Dyer's Cove
beautiful so beautiful
a challenge to the brush
of Homer and Hopper
or even David's pen.

You stand firmly grounded
by the shore
of an ocean of memory
a sea of possibility
filled with mystery
the mystery
the mysteries of life surfacing
coming in on wave after wave
laying gifts at your feet
sea glass sparkling
colored sand polished
no sharp edges
reflecting the rocking
the lullabying of the deep.

You stand together now
side by side
yet with land between
lifted up this day
underneath the sunfilled blue sky
a day so clear it seems as if
you can see forever
the sea mist morning dew

upon your fresh young faces.

You stand together now
making promises of love
joining your lives
even as the gulls fly close
you climb the apple tree
look out over the deeper channel
knowing that the fog
will come in
pea soup fog
with its ear piercing horn
and you will depend
upon the beam
that always comes
if we wait
showing the way
to safe harbor.

You stand together now
amid the flowers
on the Crescent Beach
sea oats lavender wild pink roses
along your pathway
bittersweet
all over the place
knowing the storm
that always comes
will come
the clouds will roll
the lightning will strike
the water will rise
and crash onto the shore
but remembering that
it is always amazing
what you find

after the storm
shells
put your ears to them
hear the ancient sound
sand dollars
you are rich in them
weathered wood
pieces of traps
rigging and ropes
starfish that regenerate
starfish that regenerate.

You stand together now
hearing the Voice of the Poet
at Casco Bay
seeing Portland Head Light
on a clear winter night
believing that the sun
will rise over the water
bluer than the sky again
the horizon will be so clear
you can almost see France
and you will feast
with Walter Cronkite
at the table prepared for you
at the Lobster Shack
as Mr. Ledbetter calls out the
names
of the Lobstermen.

You stand now *brilliant*
on the shore
of your life together
illumined by the lamps
of the generations

gone before you
the sun moon stars
in their courses above.
In such faithfulness
may you live
so that someday
at ebb tide
after you have received
the secrets of the sea
you will stand together still
sharing the sunset spectacular
at Kettle Cove.

You are our *Two Lights*
anchored in the Rock Eternal
distinct and wedded
A Holy Union of Light
Light of the World
Let your light so shine...

You are our *Two Lights*
shining in One Love
encircled by the Light Divine
set on a hill
for all to see
on a lampstand
giving light
to all in the house
Light of the World
Let your light so shine...

Glorify...
Glorify...
Amen and Alleluia.

Christie Smith Stephens

Blessed by Hope

*H*ope is a necessary concern in living, for in some situations we face only a confident expectation of some desired good that can sustain our spirit, helping us to see beyond them. The need for hope is structured in the human spirit, thus one of the Biblical Proverbs tells us, *"Hope deferred makes the heart sick, but a desire fulfilled is a tree of life"* —Proverbs 13:12

The Christian scriptures seek to guide our thoughts toward the highest hope—salvation, and to center our faith on the surest ground for hope—Jesus Christ. Because of Jesus, the believer is blessed by the *"hope of glory"* —Romans 5:2, Colossians 1:27, the *"hope of eternal life."* —Titus 1:2 The believer can engage in a rejoicing inspired by hope (Romans 12:12), and live a right life based on hope (Galatians 5:5). This highest hope is described as *"a living hope."* —I Peter 1:13 This highest of possible hopes means blessing. It connects us with the salvation, security, and fulfillment God wills for our life.

Hope is a necessary concern in a well-intentioned life. Hope enables us to remain sure-footed, and to keep a forward and courageous view as we live. Hope nourishes the human spirit, granting confidence and courage. Napoleon was right when he wrote this among his *Maxims,* "Courage is like love; it must have hope for nourishment."

James Earl Massey

"We have this hope as an anchor for the soul, firm and secure. It enters the inner sanctuary behind the curtain, where Jesus, who went before us, has entered on our behalf. He has become a high priest forever, in the order of Melchizedek."
—Hebrews 6:19

White River Light Station
1875

near Whitehall, Michigan

The Beacon

The beacon shines
and illumines,
stretches forth beyond the breakers.
Circling around
her Peugot Sound;
it casts its glance t'ward safer ground.

Adrift at sea
like Boston's tea,
she carries weight and starts to sink.
Light glows brighter
deep inside her;
she digs down, becomes a fighter.

Treading after
joy and laughter,
swiftly swim to warmer waters.
Fixes her gaze
to beaming blaze,
and floats with ease, cease to amaze!

Finding the shore
she steps once more
on firmament, the Solid Rock.
The Lamp that shone
to guide her home
is set upon this holy stone.

Both land and light,
He leads with might
to bring her to a resting place.
Through gale and gust
His promise just;
To light her way to Him, He must.

Joy L. May

"If I say, 'Surely the darkness will hide me and the light become night around me,' even the darkness will not be dark to you; the night will shine like the day, for darkness is as light to you."
—Psalm
130:11-12

Muskegon South
Pier Light
1903

Muskegon,
Michigan

A Shining Light

In another time, A.W. Milne felt called to missionary service in New Guinea, near New Zealand. He knew that most of the people in the interior were primitive cannibals, yet that is where he went.

Apparently he went alone, depending on friends for help with expenses. Into that jungle he carried the Christian Gospel. Not only did he survive, he converted many of the savages. He lived and died there.

Later another missionary went to the same place, but as he began to tell them about Jesus, they said, "We know him. He lived here. He had another name. Come, let us show you." In a simple village they found a small chapel with this sign over the door: "Sacred to the memory of A.W. Milne." Nearby was a small cemetery and a grave with this inscription: "Here lie the remains of A.W. Milne. 'When he came, there was no light. When he left there was no darkness.'"...His light still shines...

T. Franklin Miller

"...let your light shine before men, that they may see your good deeds and praise your Father in heaven."
—Matthew 5:16

Grand Island
East Channel
Lighthouse
1870

Munising,
Michigan

Two Lights

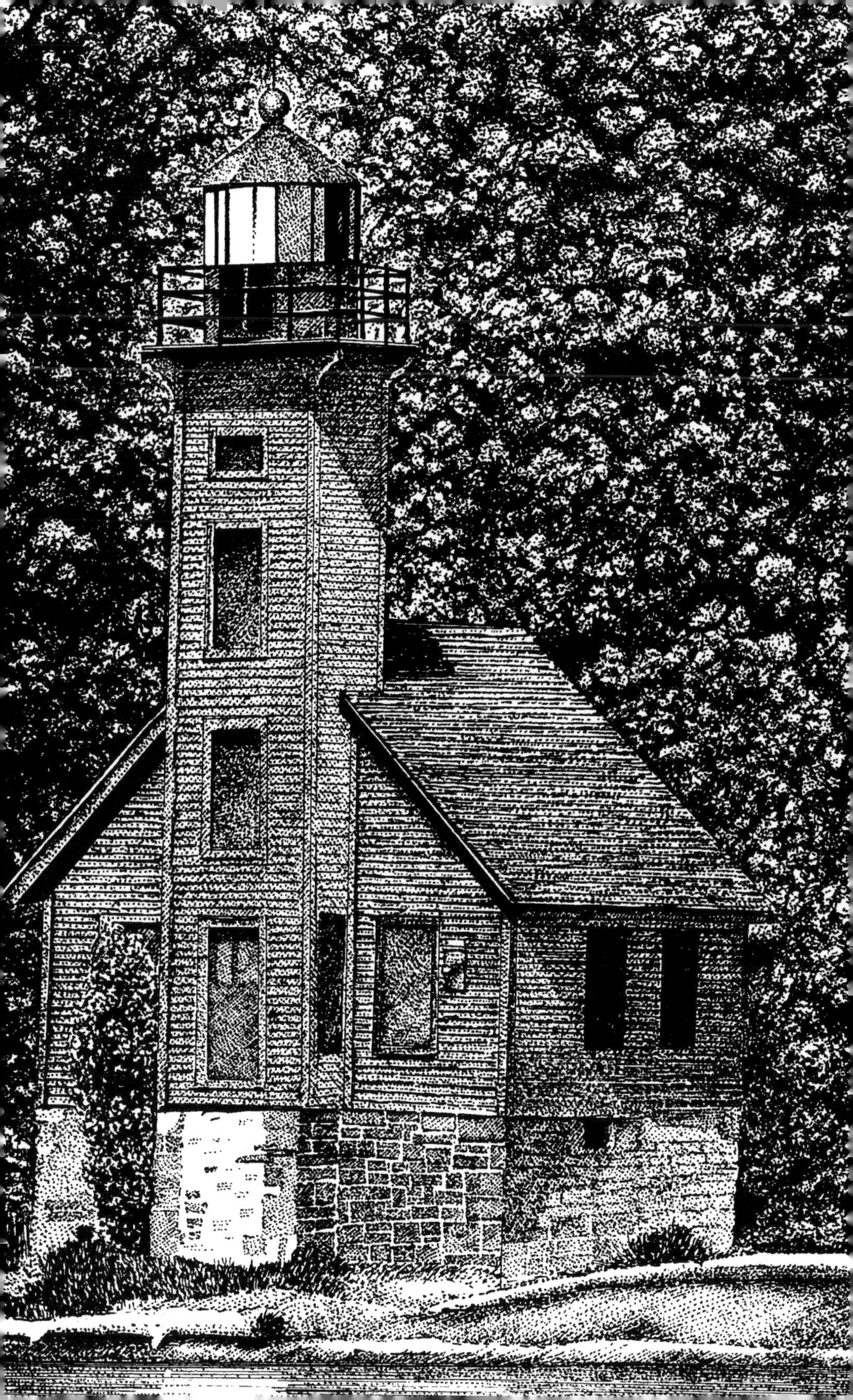

Let There Be Light

"Your word is a lamp to my feet and a light for my path. I have taken an oath and confirmed it, that I will follow your righteous laws. I have suffered much; preserve my life, O LORD, according to your word. Accept, O LORD, the willing praise of my mouth, and teach me your laws. Though I constantly take my life in my hands, I will not forget your law. The wicked have set a snare for me, but I have not strayed from your precepts. Your statutes are my heritage forever."
—Psalm 119:105-111

Seul Choix Point
Lighthouse
1805

Gulliver,
Michigan

Our daughter in Fort Wayne has neighbors who are enthralled with Christmas lights. This has been a hobby for years. They plan and create for months for new ways to display the story of Christ's birth. The house and yard are exploding with lights. We thought it was an extravagance at first but lately have been caught up with the witness. Stop, open your eyes and heart, and the meaning and spirit of light will capture you. Did not our Lord say, *"I am the light of the world?"*

I am an old timer and go back to three methods of home lighting: kerosene lamps in eastern Kentucky, gas mantles in southern Ohio and, now, electricity. I have had cataract surgery on both eyes this year. Believe me, I have pondered, in a serious way, the meaning of light and sight. They are mysteries and glories and part of God's wonderful plan.

How do the lights hit me these days? The sun and electricity are majestic but symbolize something bigger. My friend Tom Smith died yesterday, and the light of a fifty-year friendship was extinguished. Agnes and I will eat Thanksgiving dinner tomorrow with three daughters, granddaughter, and their spouses. You'll understand when we say, "They are the lights of our life."

I have had the vocation of theologian and Bible teacher, and the light of that calling still burns in my bosom. The word is *"a lamp to our feet and a light to our path."*

Notice the beautiful lighthouses around our continent, and also notice the one down the street, namely the church. Was it at a revival, a baptism, a wedding, a funeral that the light of truth and faith shone brightest for you? St. Paul invited us to *"live as children of light."* And, at last, the light of the resurrection will shine brightly on our path to eternal life.

Gene W. Newberry

Promise of Hope

"We cannot go on like this," she tells him. "I have had enough. You have promised before but the actions have not followed. You have never really cared for me. I am fooling myself to think that this marriage can make it." His defensive response is posed to counter every statement, "I can never please you. You attack me every chance you get. It is no wonder I don't come home. When I do I just get more of this same old stuff." From there it really gets ugly. During the counseling session, I usually let them see their own foibles in the process. Neither of the persons I have just described is taking any responsibility for the self or the well being of the marriage. Each has resorted to the reactive (reptilian) brain where feelings have not moved into thinking, but rather into reactive attacks, not thinking about the self but rather about the other. Blaming and defensiveness take over in automatic functioning that quickly moves them into a downward spiral. For this couple their bottom line is "no hope."

As I listen, I am reminded of the words of John 1:5. Depending on the couple's understanding of faith I might quote those profound words of hope. For me, those words have always been an uncompromising promise of hope amidst deepest darkness. A marriage in the face of its own death is a hopeless place. The ache within seems to have no balm. Nothing, absolutely nothing, seems as if it could possibly make things better. Furthermore, there are no quick fixes. It is the long arduous work of marriage to take responsibility for one's own part in the process and make incremental changes in how one functions. As if that is not hard enough, the individual must make such changes, expecting nothing from the other, but rather keeping the focus on the changes within the self. And yet it is in the work of marriage we are shaped into a different person. The light really does shine in the darkness.

Robert I. Mathis

"The light shines in the darkness, but the darkness has not understood it."
—John 1:5

Manistique East
Breakwater
Light
1917

Manistique,
Michigan

The Night the Lights Went Out

When *Life* magazine announced its picks for the century's one hundred most influential persons, a name stood out from the others. Among presidents, authors and inventors was none other than Edward L. Bernays.

Edward who?

The answer did little to convince skeptics of this man's rightful place in history or his spot on The List. Bernays, after all, was a public relations man, who worked well into retirement—he died at the age of 103—convincing people to think favorably about what he was hired to promote. Bernays was such a master of manipulation that in May, 1929, he pulled off the public relations *coup* of the century. He convinced the world to turn out its lights at precisely the same moment, wait for sixty seconds, and then, on cue, flip the switch. Let there be light.

It was a PR campaign that required months to engineer. At the center was Thomas Edison and the fiftieth anniversary of the invention of the incandescent light. To honor Edison, Bernays persuaded utility companies from around the globe to "go dark" and wait until the elderly Edison hobbled forth to re-enact his moment of invention. On the scene to witness the historic moment were President Hoover, Henry Ford, Orville Wright, John D. Rockefeller, Jr. and Madame Curie. People everywhere, in the spirit of the anniversary, doused flames, shrouded gas lamps and turned off porch lights to celebrate the moment that changed their lives forever.

A public relations *coup*, yes. But was it a "first?"

The world had been dark before. And a different kind of gift had brought a different kind of light that continues to ignite spirits, illuminate paths and change lives forever. To celebrate that moment we need no anniversary, no radio hookup, no spin doctor. "*...and there is light.*"

Holly Gooding Miller

" ..and there was light."
—Genesis 1:3

New Presque Isle
Lighthouse
1870

Presque Isle,
Michigan

The Light Still Shines

Growing up in rural America, by my eighteenth birthday I had never traveled more than two hundred miles from the farm home where I was born. While having read of the oceans in history books, I had never seen a body of water larger than a small lake. Therefore, the mentioning of a lighthouse was only imagined or read about in a book.

However, when drafted into the military, I was assigned in the Navy to the battleship, *U.S.S. Colorado,* and exposed to the wide world of water navigation and the perils of the deep. It did not take long to discover that all ships or boats, regardless of size are dependent upon the lighthouse for guidance and safety. While our ship was larger than a football field, weighed in excess of 45,000 tons, and was operated by over 15,000 people, it still needed the lighthouse as much as the tugboat or small fishing vessel. When shut in by fog or tossed about by the severity of a storm, the light from the lighthouse pierced the impenetrable darkness, helping us to avoid shipwreck on the rocky coast, enabling us to make it safely into port.

Life confronts all of us with the unavoidable severe storms of adversity. Fog gradually settles in, obscuring our vision until we are caught up in the dark night of the soul. A terminal illness, or a broken relationship, a failed business venture, or the loneliness of old age, makes it extremely difficult to find the face of God. When one can almost feel the darkness of despair, it is then that the light of God's presence breaks through. He had been there all the time, just like the lighthouse. No matter how destructive the storm or how dark the experience there is an inextinguishable Light to guide you. All of us need the Lighthouse, regardless of age, position, or power; we need the illuminating Presence of the Spirit.

Arlo F. Newell

"...The light shines in the darkness, but the darkness has not understood it."
—John 1:5

Cheboygan River
Front Range
Lighthouse
1880

Cheboygan,
Michigan

Grounded in Hope

I recognize that *hope* has been utterly foundational to my life—the very seed-bed of my existence. Why? My parents prepared that soil through their own lives. I remember little specific teaching or discussion; but I recall their positive, trust-filled lives. My father, Arthur W. Nicholson, with little formal education, was a respected Bible student and teacher.

In my early adult years, as I was working in music and editing hymnals for the Church of God, some of those hymns grabbed hold of me. My two favorite hymns both speak of the hope that is grounded in *trust in God*. God is utterly dependable:

> *Great is Thy faithfulness, O God my father;*
> *There is no shadow of turning with Thee.*

And I *am* the Lord's:

> *Whether I live or die, Whether I wake or sleep...*
> *I shall not be afraid; I am the Lord's, I know...*
> *And in the years to come, He will abide with me;*
> *I am the Lord's, I know, For all eternity.*

Or, as I have tried to teach college students over the years, using Leslie Wheatherhead's model, *God has a personal will for each of our lives:*

His *intentional* will—the ideal plan.
His *circumstantial* will—no matter what may happen.
His *ultimate* will—which in the end shall prevail.

Wonderful! These beliefs, based in Biblical truth, yield *hope!*

In this life, only people utterly grounded in *hope* are truly able to live with confidence, with Christian abandon. They have *life!*

Robert A. Nicholson

"There is one body and one Spirit—just as you were called to one hope when you were called—one Lord, one faith, one baptism; one God and Father of all, who is over all and through all and in all."
—Ephesians 4:4-5

Point Iroquios
Lighthouse
1871

near
Bay Mills,
Michigan

Searching for the Light

Suddenly it began to snow. Mother called saying to come home at once. What was to be a special evening with friends in town was cut short. This was unsettling for a sixteen year old, madly in love.

Snow during February in Kansas can be soft, gentle; and when the sun breaks through it is as if one is surrounded with thousands of glistening diamonds. Or, a storm can sweep down unpredictably with all its fury, bringing fear, even panic if one should be caught stranded alone away from home.

Street lights were only a blur. Beyond the town there was complete darkness except for the light on the falling snow directly in front of the car. My heart pounded. Could I get home before the roads became impassable?

This was a prairie blizzard. Drifts were piling higher, nearly obscuring the road. Kerosene lights in farm houses along the way did not break through the darkness.

If only I could see our barn light high above the door, then I could find my direction home. The fear that overwhelmed me must be like what a sailor experiences at sea in the midst of a hurricane searching for a signal from the lighthouse.

"...a lamp unto my feet and a light to my path." That partial scripture verse gave me hope that I would find my way home. Like a mantra, I kept repeating it aloud to break the silence and find a bit of courage.

Could the glimmer off to the north be from the barn? As the light grew brighter I suddenly saw the end of the lane that led to our house. Another half mile and I was safely home, protected from the paralyzing storm that closed us in for several days.

Hope comes to us from God's eternal Light.

Helen Jones Newell

"Your word is a lamp to my feet and a light for my path."
—*Psalm 119:105*

Charlevoix
South Pier
Light
1948

Charlevoix,
Michigan

Aunt Peggy's Rainbow

It had been a really hard time for Philip and the whole family, the kind of time we hope children will never have to face, but life has its ebbs and flows and we all get caught now and then in tidal waves that overwhelm us, currents that pull us under. If we are lucky or more than lucky, we surface, learn the lessons of the storms, to jump and ride the waves, move out of the path of the hurricane.

Philip surfaced and his mother, my Aunt Peggy, knew that her child-now-grown needed a season refreshing.

Together they traveled to Gulf Shores staying in *The Lighthouse* overlooking the Gulf of Mexico where they were calmed by the rhythmic sea at peace. A gentle rain fell as they sat on the balcony scanning the old/new horizon. Then, as if by miracle, the sun peeked through the gray mist, and right before their eyes a brilliant, full-arc rainbow lifted out of the waters rising to the skies...

Christie Smith Stephens

"Whenever the rainbow appears in the clouds, I will see it and remember the everlasting covenant between God and all living creatures of every kind on the earth."
—Genesis 9:16

Sherwood Point
Lighthouse
1883

Sturgeon Bay,
Wisconsin

Two Lights

Hope—A Given

"You gotta have hope. You gotta have hope. You gotta have hope." Over and over a television commercial repeated that refrain. This made hope sound like something we have to strain after or work up. Surely, there is more to it than that. Here are some examples:

One of the early church fathers wrote about Mary, the mother of Jesus: "She shows forth the victory of hope over anguish."

Luther, writing about Jesus as a teacher said: "He instructed me how to live and how to die and He told me what to hope for. What more do I want?"

A present-day writer reminds us that Jesus "became a symbol of hope to lepers, the blind, epileptics, the poor and dispossessed."

Paul wrote that apart from Christ we have no hope but through his shed blood we are made members of the household of God.

So, for the Christian, hope is a certainty, a given, not something we must strain after or earn.

Harold L. Phillips

"...remember that at that time you were separate from Christ, excluded from citizenship in Israel and foreigners to the covenants of the promise, without hope..."

"Consequently, you are no longer foreigners and aliens, but fellow citizens with God's people and members of God's household."
—Ephesians 2:12,19

Frankfort North Breakwater Light
1932

Frankfort, Michigan

Two Lights

Wyoming Lighthouses

One would hardly expect to find a lighthouse in Wyoming! We have the rocky landscape of the Grand Tetons and the gushing waters of Old Faithful. Neither poses much danger for ships out to sea. There would appear to be no need for the shining beacon of a lighthouse or the refuge it promises for those caught in the throws of the stormy deep.

However, there are lighthouses in Wyoming! There are people desperately looking for a ray of light in the darkness that will signal hope as they seek to return to shore from the storms of life.

My wife and I joined with eighty families in our church to become neighborhood lighthouses. We committed to a strategy of prayer, care and share to reach out with the light and love of Christ to our twenty-five closest neighbors. We pray for the presence of God to shine upon our street and into the homes through our lives. Our goal is to share Christ and the hope that He brings to those who turn to Him in the storms of life.

Recently, we were awakened at 2:00 in the morning by sirens outside our bedroom window. The light of the emergency vehicles flashed on our ceiling and walls indicating help was there for someone in need. A young woman, under the influence of alcohol, lost control of her vehicle and rammed her truck into a car parked in a neighbor's garage. My wife and I went out into the storm to comfort the family who was frightened by the early morning crash. The next day we wrote a note to share our love with the embarrassed and humiliated young driver. We offered to be there for her if she ever needed a friend.

Yes, there are lighthouses in Wyoming! There is one on our street! May the love and light of Christ radiate from it to those without hope. May all who know the *refuge and strength* that God offers stand tall and radiate His hope, His light and His life onto the shores of our neighborhood!

Milo D. Miller

"God is our refuge and strength, an ever-present help in trouble."
—Psalms 46:1

Port Sanilac
Lighthouse
1886

Port Sanilac,
Michigan

Hope and a Clock

For nearly four decades a five-foot, old Seth Thomas clock has been hanging proudly on a wall in our home. It's not a beautiful clock with an ornate polished wood finish. It's very plain with a varnished oak case and a clear glass door. The big face is easily read with its bold, Arabic numbers. Our pride in the old clock comes from the fact that it was salvaged from the Whitefish Point Lighthouse on Lake Superior. It was being replaced with modern, electronic equipment.

In its own way it reminds us of hope. Hope is like the often neglected "middle sister" in the faith, hope and love trio. Lacking the radiance of the lighthouse's beaming light and without the clamorous sound of the foghorn, the clock ticks quietly on with its task of time-keeping. Its purpose is utilitarian not attractiveness.

Unfortunately, Biblical hope has been trivialized by its common use in every day conversation like "I hope it doesn't rain today" or "I hope our team wins." It's an expression of a desire for something that has no basis in the Scriptures. In a similar vein true hope is not to be equated with optimism. While optimism is a positive attribute, it lacks the power of spirit-directed hope.

The "Good News" is that we are empowered by true hope. It is God's invitation to place our trust in His faithfulness and unchanging promises. Hope is our earnest aspiration not to give up when life seems too much for us. Hope is *an anchor for the soul."* —Hebrews 6:19 It takes the long view of life safely entrusted in the capable hands of our infinite Lord.

Hope must be nurtured. It is not a one time acceptance of God's promises. Like our lighthouse clock which must be wound once a week or it will stop time keeping, it is a continual reaffirmation of His gracious gift. The joy is that as we stay close to God with daily devotions and prayers, our hope is sustained by His loving presence.

Hollis and Elizabeth Pistole

"May the God of hope fill you with all joy and peace as you trust in him, so that you may overflow with hope by the power of the Holy Spirit."
—Romans 15:13

Whitefish Point Light Station 1861

Whitefish Point, Michigan

Source of Our Hope

There is hope based simply on desire. I hope I have the winning number in my pocket, or, I bought the ring today and I hope she says yes. Most of us have a desire to do something, have something, find or lose something. This kind of hope may or may not be intelligent, reasonable, or within the wildest scope of possibility. It simply grows out of desire.

The Christian's hope, however, finds its promise in the Word and the Gospel. It transcends immediate desires and goes to the most profound issues of life. Is there a God? What is He like? Does He know me? Does He hear when I call on Him? Does He feel my pain?

The New Testament is a promise that the answers are to be found in Jesus Christ, God's great gift to the world. He is the source of our hope both in this life and in the next. This is why we gather on the Lord's day and sing Edward Mote's great song.

"My hope is built on nothing less than Jesus' blood and righteousness; I dare not trust the sweetest frame, but wholly lean on Jesus' name. On Christ the solid rock I stand..."

Robert H. Reardon

"We always thank God, the Father of our Lord Jesus Christ, when we pray for you, because we have heard of your faith in Christ Jesus and of the love you have for the saints—the faith and love that spring from the hope that is stored up for you in heaven and that you have already heard about in the word of truth, the gospel that has come to you."
—Colossians 1:3-6

Old Presque Isle
Lighthouse
1871

Presque Isle,
Michigan

Profound Hope

In his book, *Tell Me about the Church*, Hillery Rice inscribed these words:

"David—May you find hope in this book. I deeply appreciate you—"

Hillery, October, 1992

The following passages are excerpts from three of Hillery Rice's books and are printed here with his permission:

"And they overcame him by the blood of the Lamb, and by the word of their testimony..." —Revelation 12:11 This profound hope is vindicated in Paul's testimony: *"I have fought the good fight, I have finished the race, I have kept the faith."* —II Timothy 4:7

Personal experience convinces me that Christ relates himself to the human race more through mutual suffering than any other way. He was a man of sorrow and acquainted with grief, and if we are to be His disciples we must follow His steps. Paul comprehended the imperativeness of suffering when he said, *"...we also rejoice in our sufferings, because we know that suffering produces perseverance; perseverance, character; and character, hope. And hope does not disappoint us..."* —Romans 5:3-5

No day in recorded history did tragedy so sit in the saddle as it did on the day Christ was crucified. His disciples loved Him, followed Him: their hope—all of it—was anchored in Him.

Today on the white cliffs of Dover, England, may be seen the sturdy shell of a stone lighthouse built in the year 33 A.D. by the Roman invaders. That lighthouse was constructed about the time Jesus was encouraging His followers, *"Blessed are the pure in heart, for they will see God."* —Matthew 5:8

Hillery C. Rice

"...I am the light of the world..."
—John 8:12

"But take heart! I have overcome the world."
—John 10:33

Roman
Lighthouse
"Pharos"
33 A.D.

Dover,
England

Keeping Hope Afloat

Life has a way of dashing our hopes—as emphatically as a cement block dropped on a piece of peppermint candy from the hundred and second story of the Empire State Building. I would estimate that my own longings and fervent expectations have been pounded, puréed, and pulverized almost as many times as Wily Coyote has been thwarted in his efforts to snare the key ingredient in a roadrunner casserole.

Especially in my younger days, I tended to wish for things that were improbable and of questionable importance: a jump shot like Larry Bird's, a bank account like Bill Gates's, a profile like Robert Redford's, a nose with dimensions slightly smaller than an aircraft carrier. Of course, I was as likely to realize these "hopes" as I was to sprout wings and fly nonstop from New York to Paris (while offering full food and beverage service).

Is it any wonder that fate seemed to repeatedly scuttle my dubious desires with the ease of a torpedo sinking a bathtub boat? I was relying on the spiritual equivalent of the *Titanic* to keep my hopes afloat.

Centuries before the advent of best-selling books promising to help us fulfill all our dreams, the psalmist recognized something we would do well to remember. In Psalm 42:5, the writer succinctly offers the only feasible antidote for a soul that is downcast in the midst of human longing, striving, and inevitable disillusionment: *"Put your hope in God..."*

The high-wattage flash of earthly achievement and notoriety will fade. Only God's eternal beacon of hope can bring us home, safe and alight with lasting joy.

Samuel D. Collins

"Why are you downcast, O my soul? Why so disturbed within me? Put your hope in God..."
—Psalm 42:5

Jupiter Inlet
Lighthouse
1860

Jupiter, Florida

Hope—The Light

Hope keeps us alive, often when there doesn't seem to be much else to sustain us. We often say, "I hope and pray that..." We hope; therefore, we pray. The Hebrew prophets can teach us about hope and the way that prayer demonstrates its reality.

When the prophet, Jonah disobeyed and ran from God's assignment, he found himself going down, down, down into the depths of the sea, an image of utter despair. In the lowest moment, in the belly of a large fish at the bottom of the sea, he remembered Psalm 88:6, and he uttered a prayer of thanksgiving. He said, *"When my life was ebbing away, I remembered the Lord."* —Jonah 2:7 In the middle of despair, hope was born.

The prophet, Habakkuk, was wrestling with the profoundly disturbing problem of why a loving God would allow the wicked to prosper while the righteous were suffering greatly. Habakkuk was able to express a deep faith in the mercy and care of God. Even when life's circumstances were crushing in, hope was born, and the prophet prayed. Hope came to these prophets in the middle of the night; it did not wait until the dawning. An octogenarian I have met recently loves to say, as the winter solstice approaches, "I am really excited today. There are only so many days until the days start getting longer."

Several years ago, in Portland, Oregon, a young man, attempting to take his own life, drove a hundred and fifteen miles per hour directly into a church wall. He ended up in the middle of the sanctuary, miraculously surviving. The pastor of the church, a good friend of mine, was interviewed by the press. My friend said to the reporter, "Tell everyone that we are more open for business than usual."

Hope does not wait for the good to come. Real hope is what we have in the middle of the dark tunnel; it is not only the light that comes at the end.

Fredrick H. Shively

"Though the fig tree does not bud and there are no grapes on the vines, though the olive crop fails and the fields produce no food, though there are no sheep in the pen and no cattle in the stalls, yet I will rejoice in the LORD, I will be joyful in the God my Savior."
—Habakkuk 3:17

Mendota Lighthouse
1895

Lac La Belle, Michigan

Hope Offers a Choice

Victor Frankl was a great psychiatrist. He was captured by the Germans in World War II and sent to the concentration camp called Auschwitz. After many days of cramped quarters in train boxcars he arrived at the camp. He wrote, "What a contrast as we got off the train. We were dirty and unshaved. The soldiers were spotless and clean. We had no idea of what was to occur. One man was standing right where we would get off and was pointing his finger in the direction we should go. The ten percent who went to the left had their lives spared." Frankl continued, "How absurd it is that one individual by the mere motion of the finger in one direction or the other could have control over a person's life."

There was little hope.

Sometimes we wonder if there is not some kind of "destiny determinator" who by the flick of the finger says, "You have hope or you don't." There are times we feel so helpless, faced with little hope for the future.

Perhaps one important thing to remember when everything seems hopeless is we still have a choice. Frankl had a choice. Jesus had a choice as He faced Calvary. When everything seems beyond our control and hope is gone, we too have choices.

There are times in crisis situations that bring about resources of which we were never aware. When hope seems gone it can call us to look deeply within and call for strengths and gifts we didn't even know were there. The Lord Jesus Christ knows how we grow in spiritual maturity during those times of crisis when we call upon Him. We have the choice to look down deep inside ourselves in the inner soul and bring forth resources to cope with the most difficult situation. Frankl did at Auschwitz.

When seemingly all hope is gone, Jesus who gave Himself for you and loved you will keep His word. He will help to see you through.

Charles R. Shumate

"And our hope for you is firm, because we know that just as you share in our sufferings, so also you share in our comfort."
—II Corinthians 1:7

Sturgeon Point
Lighthouse
1870

near Harrisville,
Michigan

Starfish—A Song

Starfish Starfish
Star of the Sea
Tell us your secret
Reveal the mystery.
When you are broken,
Torn apart
How do you heal,
Restore your star?

Is it a believing you can be whole?
Is it an anchoring of body in soul?
Is it a spiraling of DNA?
Is it a choosing the better way?

Starfish Starfish
Rise from The Deep
Tell us how, Show us now
Your power we need.
Sea Star Sea Star
Send out your light
Shine near and far
Lead to New Life.

One in Need
Now Receive
The Gift of the Sea Star
Regenerate Illuminate
New Life Create.

World in Need
Now Receive
The Gift of the Sea Star
Regenerate Radiate
Follow The Star.

                    Christie Smith Stephens

"...See, I am
making all
things new."
—Revelation 21:5

Potawatomie
Lighthouse
1858

Rock Island,
Wisconsin

158

This Lighthouse of Mine

He stood at the edge of the Mississippi—this lighthouse of mine. A young girl—perhaps five or six at first—proudly held her grandfather's hand. This was their time—just theirs. He stood on the river's edge pointing far up the rushing water past St. Louis to the beginnings of the wide stream. "It's so narrow," he said, "you can step across it." He spoke to her about other beginnings—his, hers, the family they shared. He connected all life to a beginning. Just as the river began—so did they—so tiny and insignificant with so much potential. He pointed across the river to tell of its history. He spoke of Indians crossing, trusting, losing their lives in a Trail of Tears. He talked of the river and the God who created it. They watched tug boats and barges on their way up to the wonders of St. Louis or down to the dream of New Orleans. He witnessed; she listened.

He shed his light. He shed it on stories, the Bible, history, music. His light spread into the darkest corners of her heart and lit it with the same light that burned in him. She didn't know it at the time, but his light lit paths neither of them knew were ahead for her. When the way was dark or stormy, his light lit the way. It led her to a light much brighter even than his own.

It has been many, many years since the lighthouse stood on the Mississippi, but the light still burns in another heart—the heart of the little girl, holding her grandfather's hand. Though the lighthouse is gone, the light is never extinguished.

Janetta Hitt Slattery

" ...I am the light of the world. Whoever follows me will never walk in darkness, but will have the light of life."
—John 8:12

Currituck Beach Lighthouse
1875

Outer Banks, North Carolina

Hope Diamond

In the Smithsonian, there is a very famous diamond on display that draws thousands of people every year to view it. It's called the Hope Diamond. It has a long and checkered history with many stories about the terrible things, the extreme bad luck, that happened to people who owned it from time to time. One story I came across may be fact or fiction. I can't prove it but it certainly caught my imagination. There was a period of time, when a woman tied the Hope Diamond on a dog and that dog walked around with a priceless jewel dangling from its neck. I can just see that diamond getting all covered with Alpo and dog drool.

Sometimes our hope gets covered over with Alpo and we begin to feel hopeless, depending on how much Alpo there is on that diamond of hope. Hope has something to do with what God is and what He is like. This kind of hope trusts God for the outcome.

And hope at its best makes it possible for faith and character to be strengthened, whatever the outcome. This extraordinary hope is contained in ordinary people like you and like me. This hope is not destroyed even when there's no possibility for things to get better. There are some circumstances in life that just are not going to get better. But this hope is not destroyed even in those circumstances. It may be covered with Alpo from time to time but it's not destroyed. This extraordinary hope is based on knowledge and awareness that there is no place you can go where God is not. Whether it's the heights or the depths or the deepest darkness, God is there. God never, never gives up on us.

God, whatever our circumstances, we invite you to dip the brush of love into the container of grace and come and take the Alpo away and send us out absolutely convinced that with you, it's possible to live in hope.

Ann Espey Smith

"May the God of hope fill you with all joy and peace as you trust in him, so that you may overflow with hope by the power of the Holy Spirit."
—Romans 15:13

Fort Niagara Lighthouse
1872

Youngstown, New York

Fast Forward

There comes a time to FAST FORWARD
Days of grief, running to and fro,
Wondering just how long we can hold out,
Leaves us weary and wanting to cry.

Then comes a time of healing, ah sweet relief,
When we just surrender and let go.
We realize that it is our nature to want to hold on.
The knowledge of having done all in our power
To change things brings a peace and calmness
That is hard to explain but easy to accept.

The flowers soon wilt, the food has been eaten,
Cards have been read, a time of loneliness appears.

Never let yourself be caught in the trap of
"If I had only done this or that."
Remember the hours, days and weeks of loving care
And be glad that you did all that you did.

Be glad that you had that loved one as long as you did.

You have been given much to remember.
So cheer up when those moments come and
Believe me, they will come.

Your family loves and supports you.
Remember that no matter how good or bad the past,
The best is yet to come.
ENJOY IT TO THE FULL.

FAST FORWARD.

Billie Roy Smith

"...weeping may remain for a night, but rejoicing comes in the morning."
—Psalm 30:5

Harbour Town
Lighthouse
1969

Hilton Head
Island,
South Carolina

Light Box Luminaries

Light is essential to healthy human life. We cannot long maintain optimal health without it. When Jesus declared himself to be the Light of the world, he gave us not only a beautiful and profound truth, but a major way of understanding what God is like.

Persons sensitive to the absence of light, may develop the medical condition of Seasonal Affective Disorder (SAD). Those afflicted sink into depression when deprived of light for long intervals, as in the dark winter months. When exposed to light again, they promptly recover.

While in the past the only recourse was to move to a sunny climate, today light boxes have been designed to treat SAD and they are often effective by simply replicating the light of dawn—10,000 lumens of light, compared to a light bulb that produces only about 300 lumens. The person simply sits in front of the light box—an excellent time for reading or crafts—for a specified time, usually a few hours each dark day.

I am exuberant in the summer with all those extra hours of light. I often sleep little while still feeling energetic. Come October, though, as the hours of sunlight shrink, so does my energy. I feel stressed, start to withdraw, stop talking. I feel weepy for no reason and could sleep much of the day and night. When my doctor recommended light therapy I purchased a light box and began to use it in conjunction with medicines to relieve depression.

The results were swift and spectacular. She also recommended two weeks in a tropical climate each winter. We chose to purchase a simple lifestyle vacation home in south Florida where SAD is unknown and there we happily vacation.

Light therapy isn't cheap, but for the many who suffer from SAD it offers hope worth its weight in gold. We cannot over-emphasize the importance of light for human well being.

Caroline Melton Smith

"...God is light; and in him there is no darkness at all."

"...if we walk in the light, as he is in the light, we have fellowship with one another, and the blood of Jesus, his Son, purifies us from all sin."
—I John 1:5,7

Cape Henry
Light
1881

Virginia Beach,
Virginia

Tick Tock, Tick Tock

A teacher shared with me that she observed a small girl in her classroom not paying attention, apparently lost in thought. Her eyes kept glancing at the clock, as though it held the key to some mysterious future. Finally the teacher intruded in her private world to see if she could learn the fast held secret. She did!

The young girl, who had overheard some distressing words in a family conversation, was totally devastated. Speaking of her father, she heard someone say, "He could die any minute." Looking at the teacher the little girl said, "And I don't know what minute that will be." All of us have had those minutes in our lives when we thought, "It could happen any time." What it was that could happen, or when it might happen, might not have seemed important to someone else.

Where do we go, what do we do, when someone brings news that seems to delete the word hope from our vocabulary? When we are told, "Sorry, that's just the way it is!" or "Wish I had better news!" where do we turn?

People move to war when there is the absence of a hope for peace. Husbands and wives contact a divorce lawyer when there is no hope for a return of the love which attracted them years before. Young people commit suicide when they lose hope that life can have significance beyond the hurts and disappointments they have experienced.

God is the source of all hope. Whatever the situation or circumstance, if God is there with you, hope is present. In calm or storm, in light or darkness, in life or death, He knows the way. Follow Him. Trust Him. Accept His joy and peace. Then you too will overflow with His hope.

Leonard W. Snyder

"May the God of hope fill you with all joy and peace as you trust in him, so that you may overflow with hope by the power of the Holy Spirit."
—Romans 15:13

Point Wilson
Lighthouse
1914

Port Townsend,
Washington

Under Her Wings

In 1979, as my father was having medical tests conducted, I was called home. It seems he slipped into a coma, then suddenly passed away. In planning the funeral service, my mother insisted on the song, *Under His Wings*. Its words speak of *balm for healing, comfort*, and a place to *safely abide forever.*

The basis of my mother's faith and hope was found in the constancy of God's providential care. To her, the light of God's love was always visible, even in the darkness of the valley of the shadow of death.

In 1988, after fires swept through Yellowstone National Park, forest rangers were assessing the damage. One ranger found a bird literally petrified in ashes, perched on the ground at the base of a tree. Somewhat sickened by the sight, he knocked over the bird with a stick, only to see three tiny chicks scurry from under their dead mother's wings. The loving mother, aware of the impending disaster, had carried her offspring to the base of the tree, gathered them under her wings, instinctively knowing that the toxic smoke would rise. She could have flown to safety but had refused to abandon her babies. Because she had been willing to die, those under the cover of her wings would live.

My mother's teaching is as steadfast: no matter the darkness or the circumstances, we can always have hope because God's care is constant.

James L. Sparks

"He will cover you with his feathers, and under his wings you will find refuge..."
—Psalm 91:4

Raspberry Island
Lighthouse
1803

Raspberry Island,
Wisconsin

Gift of Hope

When I was a child I lived with my parents for three years in a small town on the coast of Scotland. One year I was very ill and missed a great deal of school. I recovered from the illness, but I remained fragile and depressed. That spring, the daughter of our minister, Anne, a gentle, intelligent girl a few years older than I, invited me to join her on Easter afternoon in a local park for the British tradition of egg rolling. I liked and admired Anne, so of course I agreed to go.

Spring in Scotland is filled with quiet beauty. There are daffodils everywhere and the rain makes fields and lawns very, very green. I awoke on Easter, as I did every day, to the sound of seagulls in the distance. It is a noise I always associate with the bright hope of early morning.

Anne and I climbed a little green hill near her house and rolled colored Easter eggs, one right after the other, down to the bottom, and then ran after them. I was very curious about this tradition, so I asked her why they rolled the eggs instead of hunting for them. "Because the stone was rolled away from the tomb," she said.

On the Easter days to come I would remember standing beside Anne on a cold afternoon in Scotland and watching the eggs roll down like stones before us. And I would know that beauty brings with it a gift of hope and a promise that there will be another Easter and another and another and that all our days will be filled with reminders of love that we need not hunt for, but will appear to us in sweet and unexpected ways.

Gwen Spaulding-Barclay

"...in all these things we are more than conquerors through him that loved us."
—Romans 8:37

North Manitou
Island Shoal
Light
1861

near
Leland, Michigan

Scared of the Dark

I am afraid of the dark. Once in the Peruvian jungle in a night that was total darkness, I was a guest in a home overnight because a torrential rain made roads impassable. My imagination took over my thoughts, so I placed three pillows under my head and that propped me halfway up as I slept. Not great posture, but I slept.

As a teenager, I slept overnight in the First Baptist Church, having run away from home. It was dark and a church creaks and groans at night—terrifying. At another time, I was the only one in a college dormitory for dozens of nights one summer and only slept because my job totally exhausted me—eerie. One of my jobs as a teenager required me to work in the dark of night and some of the imaginative experiences of those years have entertained my children. Even today as an adult mature in years, I have frightening images when I am alone in the dark.

A little bit of light helps, just a spot of illumination from a small bulb on the bathroom wall or reflection from the stove light in the kitchen calms my fears. During a storm a small candle flame is calming and reassuring.

Dark nights have not been the only dark nights of my life. The times when I have felt I was a total failure in my vocation were pretty dark. The days when depression robbed me of ego strength were dismal. When I feared for the life and welfare of my wife and children, I was scared. At those times I recalled words from the scriptures and psychology books and quoted the following words to terrors and demons both real and imagined, either out loud or silently: *"Jesus says, I am with you always."* Those words have been a warm soft light in the dark. I still quote the words and rely on the light and hope they bring. I will tonight, if I get scared.

Oral Withrow

"The Lord is my light and my salvation—whom shall I fear? The LORD is the stronghold of my life—of whom shall I be afraid?"
—Psalm 27:1

Peggy's Cove Lighthouse
1868

Peggy's Cove, Nova Scotia, Canada

Utopian

"And we, who with unveiled faces all reflect the Lord's glory, are being transformed into his likeness with ever-increasing glory, which comes from the Lord, who is the Spirit."
—II Corinthians 3:18

I am drawn to Utopian communities,
like an insect to a buglight,
a moth to a flame;
perhaps, because I was born into
a more-than-remembrance of one,
The Church of God,
some of whose first generation,
pioneer men and women,
still walked the grounds,
still proclaimed The Word,
still sang the songs they had penned
when I was a child.
My child eyes saw them.
My child ears heard them.
My child heart took them in.

Although they no longer lived communally,
they carried the zeal of Zion in their hearts,
shaped my soul with their faith,
with their dream, with their hope that does
not die in the transitions of human constructs.

They saw The Light.
They were/are a *Shining Light*.

And so, I am a Trumpet Child,
child now more-than-grown,
knowing the complexities of existence,
the challenges of diversity,

the power of creating alternatives,
the pain of compromised vision,
the struggles of community,
but still believing,
still searching for New Harmony
making Fairhope pilgrimages,
looking for The Light,
finding it everywhere I go, for they,
the Sisters and Brothers of the Trumpet Family,
were wise enough, enlightened enough,
to focus my eyes not on the temporal,
the gray-block houses made with hands,
but on The Eternal,
The Light Not Put Out
filling my heart with its glowing beams.

The Utopian Community,
the Church that is of God,
is a Community of Spirit
Encircling, Embracing...
A Light of Faithfulness Free from Fear...

Thus, with Sister Lucena I pray,
to bear the blessed gospel light,
and with Brothers Naylor and Oldham I sing,
Shine, O shine in me.
Shine, O shine in me.

Christie Smith Stephens

Rescuing Hope

Let us first rescue this blessed word from the shallow usage as mere wishful thinking and recognize its profound meaning in God's Word. It stands for one's whole frame of thinking in the Judeo-Christian faith; the belief that life has meaning and direction; that God is on the throne; that there is a goal toward which the whole creation moves; that there is life beyond physical existence. The Hebrews believed that God would send the Anointed One; that they had a mission in the world; that God moved in history and identified with his people.

In Hebrews 6:13-19, we read *"this hope we hold as an anchor of the soul, both sure and steadfast and which enters the Presence behind the veil."* MKJV and the NEB puts it this way: *"That hope we hold. It is like an anchor for our lives, an anchor safe and sure."* An anchor for life! Thousands have found it so.

To have hope is to live in the higher "economy" of God. It is to know that we can give our all and it will not be lost and when we come to the end of our lives we will know all that we have given in the Cause of God will last into the life beyond. Dr. and Mrs. Peter Jenkins, after a career in missionary service and in healing, returned to America with little of this world's goods. They sat on the front row before me as I led a conference at a retreat in the Rocky Mountains. I had spoken of hope and cited their distinguished work as an example. Then I asked them the direct question: "Would you do it again?" Dr. Jenkins, with big tears running down his cheeks into his beard, said, "Yes, yes, yes." His lovely wife agreed fervently. They had given all and the reward was something deep in their hearts.

R. Eugene Sterner

"We have this hope as an anchor for the soul, firm and secure. It enters the inner sanctuary behind the curtain, where Jesus, who went before us, has entered on our behalf..."
—Hebrews 6:19

Port Burwell
Lighthouse
1840

Port Burwell,
Ontario, Canada

The Christmas Cactus

A few years ago, my mother gave me a cutting from a beautiful Christmas cactus that had been the pride of her mother, a grandmother I never met. In turn, my grandmother had inherited it from *her* mother, my great-grandmother of long ago. My two daughters also received cuttings, making the gift of the Christmas cactus one that stretched across five generations.

The Christmas cactus flourishes only during the winter. It is easy to forget about it during the non-blooming months; it is rather dull and lifeless looking, symbolic of winter itself. In fact, the Christmas cactus has often represented the "winters" of my own life. Once, during an overwhelming time of grief, I noticed the Christmas cactus. In my despair, I focused only on loss; likewise, the cactus was withering, even ugly. I prayed and longed for some sign of hope and affirmation. A few days later, I noticed a few brilliant, gorgeous pink "dots" on the cactus reminding me how God had graced my family. The beauty and abundance of the cactus brought hope and gratitude in the midst of grief, a symbol that life faithfully springs forth from beneath the frozen earth every spring.

But the faithful cactus also brings another kind of hope: as a "member" of our family for well over 100 years, it is obviously a survivor, and I like to associate it with the strong women in my family. It has been nurtured by a great-grandmother who bravely survived the perils of immigration; a devoted, amazing grandmother who raised six children as a farmwife during the depression, all the while caring for an invalid husband; a gentle mother who lovingly created an environment of grace, art and beauty in which to raise her family; and two strong, wonderful daughters who have begun their adult years with courage and creativity, even in the midst of difficulties.

I am grateful for the hope of the Christmas cactus!

Sue Miller Spaulding

"...I am the light of the world. Whoever follows me will never walk in darkness, but will have the light of life."
—John 8:12

"Now faith is being sure of what we hope for and certain of what we do not see."
—Hebrews 11:1

Brackley Beach Lighthouse

near Cavendish, Prince Edward Island, Canada

Faith, Hope, and Love

Medieval theologian Thomas Aquinas placed hope alongside faith and love as the three "theological virtues." He called them "theological" because God is their reference point and source. Faith, hope and love rightly order our lives in relation to God; that we display them in any degree is due to God's gracious infusion of them into our lives. But what is the relationship between them? Which, if any, precedes the other? Since faith, hope, and love are ours only by the grace of God and faith is our response to that grace, that virtue generates hope and love. But the Apostle Paul says that love is the greatest of the three, so Thomas identifies love as the mother of all Christian virtues and their form. What then of hope, the middle child in this divine trio?

"Hope does not disappoint us," says Paul. Our hope will not be disappointed—neither in this life nor the next. Hope is the virtue that orients our lives confidently toward the future. Of course the future is unknown and thus filled with uncertainty. The only sure thing about our earthly future is that it is finite, limited by the great mystery called death. In the face of the future's massive uncertainty hope stands as God's great "nevertheless."

God's goodness and constancy ultimately circumscribe the future. The poet Dante, himself a careful reader of Thomas' theology, says that the future and its element of chance touch our lives only within the larger sphere of God's providential love. In that love there is no shadow of turning. It shines with unfailing constancy to mark our way. Hope is the compass that steers our lives according to that eternal light.

Merle D. Strege

"And hope does not disappoint us, because God has poured out his love into our hearts by the Holy Spirit, whom he has given us."
—Romans 5:5

Split Rock
Lighthouse
1810

near
Castle Danger,
Minnesota

Faith and Hope

God's promise that *"...faith is being sure of what we hope for..."* —Hebrews 11:1 is the assurance that faith is no leap in the dark. Faith is the reality that God has spoken and that things unseen are as real as things that are seen. We can be certain of things we do not see.

Abraham's faith was not a roadmap showing him every turn in the road to his ultimate destination. He knew not "where" nor "what," he only knew in "whom." The one thing he knew for sure was that God was who He said He was, and that He would do what He said He would do.

My favorite Norman Rockwell painting hangs over my desk. A bearded old man with bent back rests his hand on the shoulder of a young lad, as they gaze over the horizon at a ship with full mast. All else is left to our imagination. Was Rockwell illustrating Henry Van Dykes' *Parable of Immortality?* Is the ship getting larger and larger and they say, "Here she comes," or is it getting smaller and smaller and they say, "There she goes?"

Faith and hope rest in the calm assurance that when we say "Good-bye" here we will say "Good morning" up there. Faith and hope are not promises of health or wealth. There's no guarantee that the wind will always be to your back. But there is a sure knowledge that "He will never walk alone...even through the valley of the shadow of death."

As a child places his hand into the hand of a loving earthly father, never doubting the father's love, nor questioning the destination, so we too can place our hand into the hand of God, knowing that He is who He says He is, and that He will do what He says He will do.

Paul A. Tanner

"...faith is being sure of what we hope for..."
—Hebrews 11:1

Point Prim
Lighthouse
1847

near Eldon,
Prince Edward
Island, Canada

184

The Life-Saver

Treasure-laden
Promise-making
Fortune-granting
You stand there on the sea cliff beckoning
Waving your light arms
Drawing my attention.
Suddenly the crash of waves on rocks draws me
    back to the present.
Hard to port!
Pull the rigging!
Watch those rocks!
The spray of the waves beats in my face as
    I turn to look back.
To look back at you still standing there—
Your gaze beyond the most distant point on the horizon.
And yet smiling at me
A light smile that burns into the essence of me.
Solemn, I glance back to the sea—
The dark water rolls at the bow and the wind
    tugs at the sails.
Your light dims as I slide farther out to sea
Back to my normal ports of call.
My captain yells for my attention
But my focus is only on you.
Watching you stand stock still on the rocky cliff
The waves crashing at your feet.
I doubt that we will meet again
But if I could return to you I would
And stay on your shore and in your arms forever.
The sea beckons loudly; my captain yells louder.
A glance behind—you are a speck on the shore.
With one last look back
I remove my cap in solemn salute to you
My life-saver.

Bethany K. Warner

*"And God said,
'Let there be
light,' and there
was light."*
—Genesis 1:3

Sand Hills
Lighthouse Inn
1919

near
Ahmeek,
Michigan

186

Hope Is the Thing With Feathers

*"Hope is the thing with feathers
That perches in the soul,
And sings the tune without the words,
And never stops at all . . .*

Fort Niagara
Lighthouse
1872

Youngstown,
New York

Emily Dickinson's words came alive for me recently as I watched the birds at their feeding station just outside our kitchen window. The first hard frost of the season had occurred the night before, covering the water in the birdbath with a layer of ice. A tufted titmouse stood on the surface, apparently puzzled at the loss of his fresh water supply. A few tentative pecks on the ice seemed to convince the bird that he would be unable through his own strength to reach the water below. Some movement on my part must have caught his attention. He turned, looked directly at me, and flew up onto the window sill just inches away from my face. Although the window glass separating us prevented me from hearing him, the rapid motion of his beak confirmed his vigorous chattering.

After a minute or so, the titmouse returned to the birdbath, again looked in my direction, and continued his animated chatter. Despite all of the barriers to communication between bird and human, it was impossible to misread his intentions or to ignore the air of expectancy and hope that radiated from his tiny body. I was his hope in his time of trouble, and he was relying on me to resolve a problem too big for him to handle alone.

As I reflected later upon the incident, I wondered if I am as willing as the titmouse to look in hope to the One who is able to provide the living water which alone can slake the thirst of my arid soul.

Gibb E. Webber

A View from the Bridge

It was a dark and stormy night as the mighty *Mo* traveled north in rough water. The officer on the bridge came to the captain. "Captain, there's a light in our sea lane and they won't move." "What do you mean they won't move? Tell them starboard, right now." The signal went out, "Starboard, starboard." And the signal came back, "Starboard, yourself." The captain couldn't believe what he heard. Angrily he told the officer to signal back. "This is the mighty *Mo.* Move now." The signal came back, "This is the lighthouse."

I first heard that story on a tape by Steven Covey. It planted the image in my mind of a sturdy, immovable, and steady beacon. It suggests that a lighthouse provides direction. It also suggests a possible danger and offers safety. It shatters the darkness and presents a sense of hope.

It doesn't take much vision to see the dark and stormy world in which we live. It's full of hate and wars and rumors of war. Every country in the world has its share of crime, violence, and deadly disease. Every one of us has and will continue to experience the troubled water of personal pain and fear, sorrow and sighing. Those dark days of the soul when relationships change, possessions are lost, a home is destroyed, energy dwindles, and death triumphs. We'd like some insight and help with the question: What am I going to do now?

Jesus Christ would like to make a difference in our lives. I believe He can provide us with a light that shines and cuts through the darkness of our world. I believe He's been called *the Light of the world* because the kind of life He demonstrated to us shatters the darkness all around us and promises a hope of safety and clear vision of possibilities amid all the confusion that surrounds us. In a real way Jesus Christ says to us: Follow My life and light and see what God has in store for the dark days.

William A. White

"...I am the light of the world..."
—John 8:12

"...light has come into the world, but men loved the darkness instead of light because their deeds were evil."
—John 3:19

Bodie Island Lighthouse 1872

Outer Banks, North Carolina

Light of Her Life

Lately I've been thinking about what it means for our eyes to be the lamps of our bodies. The eyes often reveal the soul, the inner person. Often they give us a clue to the real feeling or thought of those around us. We look to the eyes to see if a person recognizes, understands, approves, or loves us.

Take my mother, for instance. Her eyes characteristically twinkled when she smiled. In fact, her whole face lit up. The inner light of Christ's love shined out through her face as well as her life. Then Alzheimer's Disease struck her body. As her illness progressed, some of its effects were profound. One effect that jarred me was the emptiness in her eyes. It seemed as if the light behind my mother's eyes was being snuffed out.

Where was the "light" of her life? After all my mother's many years of following Christ, had He abandoned her now and left her in darkness? I clung to the promise that Christ would never leave her. Now and then throughout those last months, I received confirmation of that promise. Mother might hear a hymn tune and sing a few words or get tickled and break into a merry laugh or thank someone for a service done for her. The disease may have covered the light up, but it could not put the light out.

My mother knows no darkness now. She walks in total light with the Light of the world. How her eyes must twinkle!

Kathleen Davey Buehler

"Your eye is the lamp of your body. When your eyes are good, your whole body also is full of light..."
—Luke 11:34

"...I am the light of the world. Whoever follows me will never walk in darkness, but will have the light of life."
—John 8:12

Cape Lookout
Lighthouse
1859

Outer Banks,
North Carolina

Regaining Hope

"Yet this I call to mind and therefore I have hope:
Because of the LORD'S great love we are not consumed, for his compassions never fail.
They are new every morning; great is your faithfulness."
—Lamentations 3:21-23

Our journey toward regaining hope began around the time we were forced to bury our Hope. Our first child, a daughter, was born several months premature and lived about fifteen minutes. We had planned to name her Hope. However, we could not—we named her Dominique, "belonging to God." In the midst of the most painful days of our married life, something in both of us would not allow us to bury our "Hope."

The next several years brought more challenges. When we gained the courage to try again to start our family, we faced the pain of infertility and medical complications. Unfulfilled dreams, unanswered questions and countless doctors' appointments seemed to reopen the fresh wounds of grief. Meanwhile, we were dealing with Joani's father's terminal illness. He was entering the final stages of leukemia. It was watching him face death that brought healing to us. His ability to embrace a faithful God in the midst of *his* unanswered questions helped us do the same.

We have fond memories during Dad's final months of talking about faith issues. His continual statement struck us both—"God is so good." It was amazing to hear those words from a man on his deathbed. These often late-night conversations were life changing and refocused our thoughts and hearts. Two months after Dad's death, medical science and the grace of God helped us achieve pregnancy again. After a high-risk pregnancy, our first son Jonathon, named after Joani's dad, John, was born. Another difficult pregnancy brought our second son, James, as well. We have never forgotten the lessons learned in facing uncertainty. We continue to face the reality that life is hard. However, God is a faithful God who walks with us in hope.

Joani and Brent Brandon

Block Island North Lighthouse *1867*
Block Island, Rhode Island

Out of Ashes

"Do not store up for yourselves treasures on earth, where moth and rust destroy, and where thieves break in and steal. But store up for yourselves treasures in heaven, where moth and rust do not destroy, and where thieves do not break in and steal. For where your treasure is, there your heart will be also." —Matthew 6:19-21

Standing ankle deep in ashes and fallen insulation, my friend, Bill Soetenga was helping me go through my books to see what might be salvaged. Bill was a mess. His face and hands were smudged; his clothes would probably never come clean. I must have looked about the same.

From childhood, I have loved books. I like to own them. Libraries are okay, but you have to take the books back. Over the years I had filled my shelves and almost everywhere else with books I loved. From L'Amour's westerns to Kasseman's commentary on Romans—I loved them all.

Now most of them were gone, not to mention the rest of the house. Fire and sixty-mile-an-hour winds and the 38,000 gallons of water the fire department pumped into the inferno created a total loss of what had been our home. I was mourning my books. Most were marked with my notes in the margin and my favorite passages underlined. Even now, when I am writing or preparing to preach, an idea will come to mind and I will know what book and where that book was on the shelf, but they are gone...

Grief at losing books may seem strange when a home burns, but books don't long remain in print. They are not easily replaced and they become old friends, familiar and comforting. I do not like to loan my books. Some of them, in fact, I would not loan. Fortunately for me, my friends are much nicer. Books began to arrive. Some friends gave their own treasured volumes. The great British author C. S. Lewis did not like to loan his books either—until he realized that the only books we will have in heaven are those we gave away or loaned. Not literally true, but spiritually true.

Now, I loan my books. I've even given beloved books away. The generosity I received from friends helped me become less stingy. The chains of owning possessions, even books, have weakened. My shelves are full and my heart is grateful. Hope rises not from possessions, but from giving.

"Lay not up for yourselves treasures on earth where moth and rust corrupt and thieves break in and steal (or fire burns), *but lay up for yourselves treasures in heaven,...for where your treasure is, there will your heart be also..."* Would you like to borrow a book?

Richard Willowby

Almost Without Hope

"God," I cried, "I desperately need your direct guidance! Let me leave this place! I can not cope with this church's problems any longer. I'm almost without hope."

This was my prayer month after month. My ulcer caused constant pain, keeping me awake for hours, until I fell asleep. Then at 4:00 AM on a Thursday, I was suddenly awake. A magnificent clear inner voice filled with love and authority said, "Charles, you have no right to worry."

Thoughts and scriptures flooded my mind. I wrote and wrote and then I was immersed in a peace that was beyond my understanding. Was this God's direct guidance or was my mind playing tricks on me because of constant stress?

I took all the notes and put them in my Sunday suit coat. In my other coat pocket I placed my sermon manuscript. I was torn between using my sermon or sharing this experience on Sunday. The answer came from a most unexpected source—a smiling, loving elderly lady, Betty Trick. She did not teach or preach. She prayed.

She became living proof that *"The eye cannot say to the hand, 'I don't need you!' And the head cannot say to the feet, 'I don't need you!' On the contrary, those parts of the body that seem to be weaker are indispensable, and the parts that we think are less honorable we treat with special honor...God has combined the members of the body and given greater honor to the parts that lack it."* —I Corinthians 12:21-24 Greater honor was given to a less significant saint.

"Pastor," said Sister Trick urgently, "I must talk to you before worship. You were in terrible trouble Thursday night at 4:00. I was suddenly awake and prayed for you for about thirty minutes. Then a great peace settled over me. Oh yes, God gave you a message for today and you are supposed to preach it."

Just as towering lighthouses guide ships, God sometimes guides us through His voice within us and through the "least" of those in His Body.

Charles N. Moore

"Turn your ear to me, come quickly to my rescue; be my rock of refuge, a strong fortress to save me. Since you are my rock and my fortress, for the sake of your name lead and guide me."
—Psalm 31:2-3

"For this God is our God for ever and ever; he will be our guide even to the end."
—Psalm 48:14

Forty Mile Point Lighthouse
1897

near
Rogers City,
Michigan

Perfect Timing

Divorce. Death. Darkness. How can anything good come from such places of despair? I thought my marriage would last a lifetime. David felt the same way about his. But, it didn't happen for either one of us. After twelve years of trying, my marriage ended in divorce. David's ended when his wife was taken by cancer.

We had known each other for a long time. I was his deacon and friend. I walked the valley of death with him and we both believed that somehow all things would work together for good. We knew God surely had a plan.

We became closer as time went on and it wasn't long before we fell in love. The light had come to both of us at the same time! We were making wedding plans when David, out of a heart of love for lighthouses and me, wrote the following letter. From a devastating divorce, an untimely death and paths of darkness, we were led into an experience of light and hope.

"You have turned on my light! The LORD my God has made my darkness turn to light...What a God he is!...All his promises prove true."
—Psalm 18:28-20

Sand Point
Lighthouse
1867

near
Escanaba,
Michigan

"Risë, you are the lighthouse of my life! When we first met you became a lighthouse on the shore of my life. It was nice and pleasant just knowing you were there. Over the next months, I watched and experienced the way your light spread and helped so many people.

When my waters became troubled and stormy, you became a beacon that offered hope and salvation. When times became their blackest and heaven opened, you were there for me. You helped keep me away from the rocks of destruction.

Later, I became interested in the light itself. This light now shines throughout my entire life. It has helped me feel alive again and has provided a new direction. I know that you have built your lighthouse on a solid rock. But, if and when your light needs recharged, refocused, repaired or just given a rest from the pressures of the world, know I will be there for you. Just ask. I love you, now and forever, David"

Yes, God had a plan...and His timing is always perfect!

Risë and David Singer

A Shining Moment

"But for you who fear my name, the Sun of Righteousness will rise..." —*Malachi 4:2*

Morning came, more often than not, cloaked in a gray, soft blanket. The fog rolled up from Puget Sound, the overcast fell as if a drape from the sky, and the breaking of day arrived with the hushed quiet and half-light of a Seattle mist. The damp glistened on the pavement, on the dark green leaves of rhododendrons, and the camellia bushes, heavy with pink blossoms. The fresh scent of saltwater, mixed with evergreen, spoke of life, as I walked to school in those days, glistening in my yellow rain coat, the kind all boys and girls used to wear.

Of course, many people imagine that Seattle's weather is gloomy and dull. Depressing. Hopeless. But, growing up there, I never found it so. The overcast strangely comforted me. It forced me to study each tree and bush individually, as they were revealed, one-by-one, instead of passing by everything at once. Chestnut trees would take shape, gradually. The camellias, on the other hand, appeared almost suddenly.

The minutes would grow brighter, as light wrestled with the clouds and the sun moved toward noon. Still gray, the sky seemed to come alive, revealing currents of fog and shafts of light, shifting, changing, forming, flowing.

After a while, you learned to watch as the sun broke through. Sometimes by lunchtime. Sometimes by the end of the recess. Sometimes not until the day was almost gone, just before dinner. A brief, shining moment.

Life is so much like that. We see things, as if through a fog. the mist shrouds what's up ahead. And, strangely, that helps us to see: more accurately, more closely. We notice the details, the small things, the big things, one-at-a-time.

We learn to expect the sun. Even when overcast, when others are without hope, we hope for, we expect, the sun to break through. Others whine, wait. Others despair, we watch thoughtfully. Others can't see, we close our eyes and breathe the fresh scent of saltwater, tinged with evergreen. We, by faith, glimpse the light prevailing, noticing how much brighter the day has become. We know that the sun will shine, even if but for a moment, at the end of the day.

And that makes the half-light of morning all the more hopeful. All the more certain to grow brighter as life unfolds.

James D. Lyon

 Mukilteo Lighthouse, Puget Sound *1906*
Mukilteo, Washington

How Can I Write About Light?

How can I write about light
when the stars hide behind
big, ominous clouds and the moon
is nowhere to be seen,
when the twinkling is but a memory
of a time when the realities of life were
less apparent and the tenets of faith
rolled more easily off the tongue?

How do I write about hope
when we are crushed with the
news of earthquakes taking thousands
leaving a wailing without solace,
the desperate cries of survivors
wondering why,
when our children walk into schools
with assault weapons
and fire upon our children,
when religious folk continue to war
with religious folk in the name of God,
when so many starve
aching with hungers
for so many reasons never filled,
when old people linger
in nursing homes way
beyond their seeming wishes,
when the young and not so young
die inch by inch while praying
to be spared,
when oppressions prevail in spite
of our efforts to change the world,
when the old hurts of my life will not

be quieted by understanding or forgiveness,
when healing is as illusive as prevention
and justice and mercy have failed
to roll like mighty waters?

How do I write about light and hope
with any kind of integrity,
without sounding, without being,
a cymbal clanging?
Have I not lived too long for the
comfort of placebos
and yet have I not lived too long,
seen too much, to indulge so foolishly
in cynicism and despair?

I write about light
in the face of such absence
for light will not leave me alone.
It shines in the center of my soul
begging for/requiring my tending...

I write about hope
in the presence of such anguish
for hope will not leave me alone.
It calls my name, puts the pen
in my doubting/believing hand,
bids me send the signal of
things once seen, remembered...
things unseen yet strangely believed...
the light not put out.

Christie Smith Stephens

Who Can Live Without Hope?

"Who can live without hope?" asked the poet Auden. The obvious answer is, no one. Persons from whom everything else has been taken have survived on hope alone. On the other hand, one who has unfathomable wealth but is without hope will find life not worth living. So what is this thing that we cannot live without?

Michael Downey writes, "Hope is precisely what we have when we do not have something. Hope is not the same thing as optimism that things will go our way, or turn out well. It is rather the certainty that something makes sense, is worth the cost, regardless of how it might turn out. Hope is a sense of what might yet be. It strains ahead, seeking a way behind and beyond every obstacle."

As Downey suggests, hope exists only when we need it. When we are enjoying health, prosperity, love, and all life's best, hope is not even on our minds. But when our comfort is taken from us or even threatened, when trouble and tragedy come as they inevitably must, we begin to comprehend the value of this gift, as we know the value of water when the well is dry. It is born out of the vacuum of despair, coming to us when, and only when, we desperately need it.

Even though hope must exist in the present, it is more about the future than the present. It is a magnetic force that draws us into the future, giving us a reason to believe that tomorrow is worth whatever it takes to get there. It is the faint light in the darkness, the cool breeze in the desert, the hand that reaches out when we're in freefall, the recognition that the way things are now is not the way they have to be or even will be. It is the very breath of life. Truly we cannot live without it.

Kay Murphy Shively

" ...remember that at the time you were separate from Christ, excluded from citizenship in Israel and foreigners to the covenants of the promise, without hope and without God in the world. But now in Christ Jesus you who once were far away have been brought near through the blood of Christ."
—*Ephesians 2:12-13*

Cape Hatteras
Lighthouse
1870

Outer Banks,
North Carolina

Only Two Miles from Shore

A recent tragic news story told of a Greek ferry boat, named *Express Samina,* carrying over five thousand passengers, capsizing and killing at least sixty-two people. It was reported that the ferry was meandering through the Aegean Sea on its daily route when it struck a rocky outcrop only two miles from shore. The disturbing thing about this tragic accident was that it could have been easily avoided. A beacon light marking the rocks was visible for seven miles, warning all who sailed of the lurking danger. One official, in trying to explain how the ship collided with the rocks, said, "You have to be blind not to see it (the beacon light)." Upon investigation, it was discovered that the crew members were watching a soccer game on television when the ship ran aground. Murder charges are being filed against the crew.

While we may be quick to judge the crew of the *Express Samina* for their behavior in the loss of so many lives, their gross negligence serves to remind us of how easily we can be distracted from the light God has given us. Most of us would agree that God has made His light shine upon us, especially by giving us His Son Jesus Christ. One can hardly deny that we have all the light necessary for us to avoid tragedies of our own making. Like the Greek sailors, many times our difficulties in life are not a result of our *intentions* but lack of *attention.* God's light is wonderful. It will always lead us in the right direction and out of harm's way, if we keep our eyes and hearts focused toward Him.

Rodney F. Bargerstock

"The LORD is God, and he has made his light shine upon us."
—Psalm 118:27

Michigan City
East Pierhead
Lighthouse
1904

Michigan City,
Indiana

Silence of the Night

At the age of two, I died. It was the very first time I suffered an asthma attack. As the oldest daughter of poor Louisiana sharecroppers, I was the pride of their life. Now, I lay limp and lifeless in my mother's arms as Dad drove as fast as our old truck could to the nearest doctor over thirty-five miles away. My God fearing mother feverishly prayed my life would be spared. But with each bump in the rut-infested road my color told the story. I wasn't breathing and they were a long way from the doctor's office in Jonesville, Louisiana. Once there, they knew that I still might not get the help I needed in time to save my life. At that time, the white waiting room had to be emptied before any black person could be treated. Back home, my grandparents, founders of the Doty Road Church of God, humbly prayed, "Our Father, please give us our little girl back! We know you can and we believe you will!"

I was totally unresponsive when my parents pulled in front of the small-town doctor's office. It must have been divine providence, because that day, the white side of the office was completely empty. Quickly, my parents handed me over to the doctor. Then they waited. Prayed and waited. Finally, they heard a faint cry. God had given me back to them... and to the world.

I was given back, but I continued to suffer with severe asthma attacks. Many nights of lonely and silent suffering took their toll on my faith. I wondered if I was doomed to suffer. A simple treat, such as riding a bicycle with our daughters, left me gasping for breath. One night, after having given myself three shots of adrenaline and making two trips to the hospital, I had a personal talk with God. In the silence of the night, I humbly whispered, "Lord, I'm Your child. I believe that You have a purpose for my life. Heal me, or take me home with You because I can't go on like this. Either way is all right with me. Do which ever brings glory to Your name."

Back home in a country town in Louisiana, my mother continued her lone vigil of prayer. For twenty-five years, she had kept the hope that someday, I would be healed. Now, I had joined her in asking God for my healing. In the spring of 1975, we celebrated the victory. It continues to this day!

Jean Tolliver Morehead

 Pilot Island Lighthouse *1873*
Port des Morts, Wisconsin

It Was in the Kitchen

It was in the kitchen
where women often talk
telling the truth of our lives
preparing food
cleaning up the leftovers
that she told me
at our friend's urging
of her healing.

Her pink ribboned survivals,
the visit of Light in the corner,
the seeing, the hearing
the Face, the Word of Life,
her claiming that which
is difficult to believe
so risky to share
lest we be casting pearls
before oinking pigs
yet the knowing of our experience
prevails and requires
the witness.

And so it was
on a Sunday in October
in the parsonage
at Harmony Hill
three women
heard once again
the resurrection story,
felt the presence
of the holy, of salvation,
of new life in our midst.

And with Julian of Norwich
centuries before
we proclaim,
All shall be well.
All is well.

Amen and Alleluia.

for Nell Cole and Dean West with deep gratitude
Christie Smith Stephens

"Jesus went throughout Galilee,...healing every disease and sickness among the people."
—Matthew 4:23

Chambers Island
Lighthouse
1868

near
Fish Creek,
Wisconsin

You Are Lighthouses

Jesus said: *"I am the light of the world"* —John 8:11

It would not violate the meaning of the Scripture to say: Jesus is the lighthouse for the sea; those who sail by His light will not sail in darkness and sink their ships on the reefs, but will have the light of life.

And Jesus also said: *"You are the light of the world."* —Matthew 5:14. In the same spirit of interpretation we may hear Him say: You are lighthouses along the shores of the sea. Let your beam so be cast that those in peril on the sea, when they see the good you do, may give their praise to God and be drawn into the love of the heavenly Father.

Richard H. Petersen

"You are the light of the world. A city on a hill cannot be hidden. Neither do people light a lamp and put it under a bowl. Instead they put it on its stand, and it gives light to everyone in the house. In the same way, let your light shine before men, that they may see your good deeds and praise your Father in heaven."
—Matthew 5:14-16

Block Island
Southeast
Lighthouse
1875

Block Island,
Rhode Island

Permiquid Point Lighthouse

The Light in Daddy's Eyes

"...God is light; in him there is no darkness at all."
—I John 1:5

While thinking about a story that illustrated hope and light, I remembered my father's vision loss and the agony he suffered from being unable to see clearly.

Dad underwent cataract surgery in 1980 and 1984. An infection from the surgery resulted in permanently blurred vision and watering of the left eye. In 1986, Dad was diagnosed with Myasthenia Gravis. This is an autoimmune disease that results in episodes of muscle weakness of the entire body. Because his eyelids now drooped his field of vision narrowed. To try and correct the problem surgery, called "tucks" of the eyelids, was performed two or three times.

Dad and I made many trips to his ophthalmologist during those years. Each time he would climb into the office chair prior to looking at the eye charts. He always had so much hope that he would see an improvement in his vision from his last trip. The reverse was happening. Light, both artificial and natural, hurt his eyes.

One day in 1992, I took Dad to pick up his new glasses that his ophthalmologist had prescribed to try and help his failing vision. He had such great hope that those glasses would enable him to read his daily newspaper and watch his beloved Atlanta *Braves'* baseball games on TV!

As we came out of the office that day to get into the car for our drive home he told me, "I can't see." Thinking it was because his eyes had been dilated an hour or so earlier, we started our drive home. More and more he complained that he couldn't see from either eye. Thinking "stroke," I took him to our local ER. My mistake! After medical tests failed to find a cause for his sudden further loss of vision, the doctor suggested we go home, with eye drops and "let his eyes rest" overnight. His sight was still very limited the next morning.

As long as I shall live, I will remember taking him to the ophthalmologist early that morning. Dad sat down for yet another eye exam, all the while holding those new glasses, hoping and praying the drops had somehow helped his vision.

As the exam got underway and nothing could be attributed to Dad's existing illnesses, the ophthalmologist suggested yet another test. He described it to us as a bright light used to shine directly into the macula of the eye, the central and most vital area of the retina.

Dad was anxious to get started, thinking at long last he would be helped. As the extremely bright light was used, following the insertion of medicine drops in each eye, the doctor slowly lowered the light and told us in a tired voice the sad news. Daddy had suffered a sudden, painless further loss of his vision because of macular degeneration. Had we known the symptoms of the disease and gone directly to the ophthalmologist when Dad told me he had suffered the vision loss in both eyes, he possibly could have been helped, though there is no absolute cure.

From the day of that office visit, Dad and I made many more trips to his ophthalmologist. Each time he had so much hope that somehow his vision had improved. Each time the light was used in the exam. The test told us the vision was slowly worsening.

In an effort to see, Dad must have used his hands to push the glasses further up on his nose at least a thousand plus times, to no avail.

He stopped driving his little red pickup in late 1994. He had peripheral vision, but no central vision. Dad listened to his last *Braves* game as they entered the World Series on October 20, 1996. He died of a heart attack at approximately 11:30 PM. His glasses were on his nightstand.

Dad was buried with those glasses on that had represented so much hope. My thoughts were "He no longer has to push those up in an effort to see; God's light will be sufficient."

Joyce Thompson Thornton

The Sun Is Shining

My mother for nine years suffered with and overcame in various, remarkable ways Alzheimer's Disease. One of the last things she said, perhaps, the last sentence she spoke before she died was, *"The sun is shining."* Her beautiful, beautiful brown eyes, she was her daddy's brown-eyed darling, her brown eyes were closed. She had closed them because she could not die while seeing her grandchildren for they, she said, were life. The drapes in the room where she lay between the pink sheets her son, my brother, had bought for her were closed. The sun was not shining on Jones Valley in Huntsville, Alabama, that day but, as always, my mama saw the light and, as always, she testified to it.

As God did when God said, *"Let there be light,"* she created in the void, in the darkness of her leaving us, a light to shine for us, a light into the future she was glimpsing, a sunlight she was seeing and to which she gave witness. In her last hours with us physically she endowed us with hope, the hope of light, the light of hope.

The sun is shining...

Christie Smith Stephens

"And God said, 'Let there be light,' and there was light."
—Genesis 1:3

Sturgeon Bay
Ship Canal
North Pierhead
Lighthouse
1903

Sturgeon Bay,
Wisconsin

Portland Head Light

More Than Just "I Hope So"

Alone in the waiting room in the middle of the night, I knew the surgery was taking far too long to be routine. I hoped and prayed and read many scriptures. After hours that seemed like days the surgeon came to me. "Your wife had a ruptured, gangrenous appendix, which I removed. She is a very sick woman." One week later she walked out of the hospital by my side as marvelling nurses watched. One said "That lady had a ruptured, gangrenous appendix just eight days ago." Fifty-one years later I am still thanking God that my wife is still with me.

Faith in the night, joy in the morning! *"Why are you downcast, O my soul? Why so disturbed within me? Put your hope in God, for I will yet praise him, my Savior and my God."* —Psalm 42:5.

The strongest hope relies on belief in God. Paul writes, in Romans 4:18, *"Against all hope, Abraham in hope believed and so became the father of many nations, just as it had been said to him..."* Abraham's hope was not just "I hope so." He believed that God had promised him an heir when the circumstances made it seem impossible. He "believed against hope."

The Christian hope is more than just hope. It is something objective. It is trusting in what Christ has already done. He is our hope. Hebrews 6:19 makes this clear. *"We have this hope as an anchor for the soul, firm and secure. It enters the inner sanctuary behind the curtain, where Jesus...has entered on our behalf."* By his atoning death he has entered where God is so that we can follow him there. He was with God before he came to earth, but now he has returned to God with a new name, Savior.

The Christian hope is a basis for action. Count on it!

Frederick G. Shackleton

"Against all hope, Abraham in hope believed..."
—Rom. 4:18

Plum Island Rear Range Light
1897

Plum Island, Wisconsin

A Beacon of Hope in a Restless Sea

We long so much for peace and tranquility in the midst of life that seems more like a restless sea. A restless sea...

I'm reminded of a Sunday morning during worship at our home church. There we were, two families claiming most of a pew...Son, daughter-in-law and three granddaughters with Gran and Papa as the bookends. Olivia, the two year old, was especially restless—not noisy or disruptive—just restless. On the pew, off the pew. On one lap, then another. Even her teenage sisters could not entertain her long enough to calm the restlessness.

Then she was coming toward me. She climbed up on my lap. I took her in my arms and started to rock ever so gently back and forth, even humming quietly in her ear. In what seemed only a moment, her eyelids drooped, eyes closed and she was fast asleep. In the safe and comforting arms of her Papa, her restlessness ceased.

Little Jewish children, we are told, often climb upon the lap of their Father, take his face in their two little hands and say respectfully, "Abba Father." Out of this Jewish context and in the midst of his restlessness in the garden, Jesus was heard to pray, "Abba Father."

When our restless spirit turns toward God there is hope. Hope becomes the lighthouse casting its beacon of light on the restless sea of our life. Hope points us toward the safe harbor of our Heavenly Father's arms. And in His arms we can cease our restlessness and experience His peace.

Jerry C. Grubbs

"You are my lamp, O LORD; the LORD turns my darkness into light."
—II Samuel 22:29

Edgartown Harbor Light
1875

Edgartown,
Martha's Vineyard,
Massachusetts

Garden of Hope

The Plum Orchard Park on the side of the mountain above the ancient Japanese hot-spring town of Shuzenji was not at first my "Garden of Hope," even though I knew the pink and white blossoms were symbols of hope in Japan. I had gone there every year after attending an International Women's Conference in the Amagi mountains. I stayed across the valley from Shuzenji. Early the next morning I walked across the valley and up the narrow road.

Far on the horizon sat the snow-covered, cone-shaped Mount Fuji. Moved deeply by the silence, by the gifts of the pale pink, the white and deep pink flowers, and by their childlike purity, it seemed I could almost hear the blossoms singing of "hope."

That night after returning home, I dreamed of the Plum Orchard. Once again I stood in the orchard surrounded by the scent and color of blossoms.

My father called in February, 1976. My mother had had an almost fatal heart attack. My father pleaded, "Come home, Phyllis. We need to be here together."

Flying into the sun on my way to Seattle, although I couldn't understand the unexplainable timing of that dream and the morning on the mountain, I knew God's hand moved within the experience, and that the memory of it was mine forever. Arriving in Seattle, I called home. My mother would live.

After her death in November, 1989, I went again in late January to the Plum Orchard above Shuzenji. I found the orchard a frozen winter-land, the half-opened blossoms sheathed in the same ice of death I carried in my heart.

For a long time I sat there alone in the orchard. Then little by little the memories of the year the blossoms sang to me began to flood my body with warmth. I remembered that long ago scent of hope. The ice within me melted. Once again I experienced the newness of God's steadfast love that "never comes to an end."

Phyllis Gillespie Kinley

"Yet this I call to mind and therefore I have hope: Because of the LORD's great love we are not consumed, for his compassions never fail. They are new every morning; great is your faithfulness."
—Lamentations 3:21-23

Goderich Main Light
1847

Goderich, Ontario, Canada

222

Shining Lights

In recent months I have been impressed by the work of Thomas Kincaid, known as "the painter of light." Each of his paintings is infused by some focus of light which draws the attention of the viewer and gives special meaning to the painting. This special illumination has a way of bringing the painting to life.

As I think about my own life, it isn't difficult to identify those places where the light of hope came into focus through persons and made a difference in my life. My aunt Carrie who was also my childhood Sunday School teacher was able to bring the light of God's love into my life and thus translate the word of the Gospel into a warmth that encouraged the early seeds of faith to sprout and grow.

A number of people were responsible for continuing to nurture the seeds of hope through their encouragement of the growth process.

An eighth grade teacher who told me she believed in me when I didn't believe in myself was one of those persons. Her faith in me helped me through some of the difficult times in my life and became a source of hope that helped to light my way through the darkness.

I owe a debt to many people who have helped to light the path I followed in my lifetime. My task is to pass the hope on to others—to let my light shine so that they too may find their way as I found mine.

The world around us is affected by the darkness of prejudice, ignorance, and fear. As followers of Christ we are called to be bearers of the light so that others may find their way.

John W. Little

"...let your light shine before men, that they may see your good deeds and praise your Father in heaven."
—Matthew 5:16

Sturgeon Bay
Ship Canal
Lighthouse
1903

Sturgeon Bay,
Wisconsin

224

My Father's Sigh

My father's sigh lays upon my heart heavy, uncomfortable like an wet army blanket on a summer day.

Like olive drab army blankets piled high upon my chest my daddy's sighs lay on and in my heart.

Sighs of missing his wife of now sixty years, his wife called, recalled by the Creator five years ago.

Sighs of missing her here in this place of their early marriage, this place of their/our church heritage, this camp meeting ground of tabernacles, old hymns, treasured friends, this place of too precious memories of youthful bodies, trailer courts, laughter, studies, little children, struggles for survival, the still unfulfilled promise of their dreams.

My father comes here now without her, without his sweetheart at his side. He sees her everywhere. His eyes mist. He grows quiet as the multitude sings in glorious parts,

> *Whether I live or die*
> *Whether I wake or sleep*
> *I am the Lord's I know.*

He sighs with the Holy Spirit the sighs too deep for words as he remembers my mother, as he ponders his own dying. These sighs fall upon my heart, heavy almost crushing.

I miss her. We all miss her. We do not know his grief, only our own. We hate the thought of his leaving us, his not walking these grounds someday way too soon no matter how long, but we cannot give power to loss. We have so many blessings to count.

They both taught us this *no-matter-what-happens-must-sing-faith* and sing we will. Tossing off the blankets we raise our voices,

> *Nothing shall separate from this unbounded love.*
> *Nothing shall separate.*

Husband, daddy, granddaddy, great-granddaddy lifts his eyes. Comforted, he sings. She is with him/with us always. As is the One in Whom she believed, the One who delivered her, she is forever with her beloved husband, with her family always.

Sighs give way to singing. Sighs give way to singing.

Christie Smith Stephens

Manitowoc North Breakwater Light *1918*
Manitowoc, Wisconsin

I Found Hope

Nearly forty years have come and gone since I saw her last. Time seems to have taken a toll on both of us. There are some precious memories that even time cannot steal from one's heart.

I still have vivid memories of her stability, her grace, and her simple charm. These traits were all a part of her nature, and it was these traits that drew me to her.

Our first meeting was one of chance. A third party, my grandfather arranged it. It was a cold, damp and windy Sunday morning, which was rare for the state of Louisiana. At first glance I did not think very much of her. She seemed so old-fashioned, dull and boring. My grandfather and I were the first to arrive and as others gathered, she seemed to brighten up and take on a warm, friendly persona.

What stands out in my mind was the fact that from the very first meeting, she accepted me. It felt good to be accepted.

My relationship with her lasted for nearly four years. She nurtured me, instructed me and sometimes rebuked me, but never turned her back on me. This last fact was so important because growing up in the South during some of my formative years, I faced an awful lot of rejection. I was born out of wedlock, poor and black. The old adage "three strikes and you are out" seemed to apply to me.

With her I felt loved, accepted and valued. She never spoke without reminding me of how much God loved me. I found a place of comfort in her. She became my Rock of Gibraltar, my shelter in the midst of a storm. I leaned on her during some very trying times in my life and she was always there. She will always occupy a very special place in my heart.

"She" was my very first home church. I was informed that she was finally demolished in the name of "progress." Though the building is gone, the impact of her influence remains with me to this day. Inside of her walls, I found hope, the kind of hope that has made me *"more than a conqueror."*

James O. Morehead

Yaquina Head *1894*
near Newport, Oregon

Houses of Light

"And God said, 'Let there be light,' and there was light. God saw that the light was good, and he separated the light from the darkness. God called the light 'day,' and the darkness he called 'night.' And there was evening, and there was morning—the first day." —Genesis 1:3-5

What are
these houses
first-order lens lamps
placed high on stands
if not hope portraits
pen and ink drawings
to The Creator Spirit
artist's renderings of
The Eternal Soul
who from the void
spoke The Word
calling forth
The Light

And There Is Light.

Christie Smith Stephens

Contributing Writers

John L. Albright and his wife Ruth live in Sterling Heights, Michigan. He is Senior Pastor of Bethany Church of God near Detroit. John is the former Youth Director at the National Board of Christian Education of the Church of God. *(see page 18)*

Cleda Achor Anderson and her husband Joe live in Holmes Beach, Florida. She is an Associate Pastor of Longboat Key Community Church. Dr. Anderson was the first Youth Pastor at Park Place Church of God and former Dean of Students at Anderson University in Anderson, Indiana. *(see page 26)*

Gwen Spaulding-Barclay and her husband Michael live in Indianapolis, Indiana. She has taught school at the secondary level and is presently pursuing a career in writing. *(see page 172)*

Ilene Gray Bargerstock and her husband Rod live in Anderson, Indiana. She has been a pastor's wife and retired from Church and Ministry Service of the Church of God as office manager. *(see page 22)*

Rodney F. Bargerstock and his wife Ilene live in Anderson, Indiana. He is an ordained minister in the Church of God and recently retired from Board of the Church Extension of the Church of God. *(see page 200)*

Cheryl Johnson Barton and her husband Bernie live in Kobe, Japan. She is a writer and a missionary. *(see page 30)*

James W. Bradley and his wife Judy live in Ocala, Florida. He is Senior Pastor at College Park Church of God. Formerly he was the Director of Pastoral Studies at Anderson School of Theology in Anderson, Indiana. *(see page 34)*

Joani Somppi Brandon and husband **Brent P. Brandon** live in Anderson, Indiana. Joani is an Assistant Professor in Music Education at Anderson University. Brent is a Vice-President at First Merchants Bank in Anderson, Indiana. *(see page 194)*

Kathleen Davey Buehler and her husband Keith live in Anderson, Indiana. She is Children's Editor of *Bridges* Curriculum of the Church of God. Kathleen is also the author of seven books. *(see page 192)*

Barry L. Callen and his wife Arlene live in Anderson, Indiana. He is University Professor of Christian Studies at Anderson University and Editor of Anderson University Press. Dr. Callen has authored twenty-four books. He is also a former Dean of both Anderson University and Anderson School of Theology. *(see page 32)*

Samuel D. Collins and his wife Sharon live in Anderson, Indiana. He is an ordained minister in the Church of God and currently is a Staff Writer for Church of God Ministries. *(see page 152)*

James R. Cook and his wife Carol live in Columbus, Ohio. He is Senior Pastor at Meadow Park Church of God and has also pastored in Michigan. *(see page 40)*

Joseph L. Cookston and his wife Merry live in Clayton, Ohio. He is an Associate Minister at Salem Church of God near Dayton, Ohio. Dr. Cookston was the Director of Adult and Family Ministries at the National Board of Christian Education of the Church of God. *(see page 46)*

David L. Coolidge and his wife Shirley live in Anderson, Indiana. He is Minister of Music and Worship Emeritus at Park Place Church of God. *(see page 48)*

Kenneth E. Crouch and his wife Carolyn live in Muncie, Indiana. He is a minister in Eaton, Indiana, and the former Director of Admissions at Anderson University. *(see page 50)*

Ronald V. Duncan and his wife Martha live in Pasadena, Texas. He is Senior Pastor of Parkgate Community Church of God in Pasadena. Dr. Duncan is a chaplain in the National Guard with the rank of Major. *(see page 52)*

Bobby W. Dunn and his wife Jackie live in Chilhowie, Virginia. He is Senior Pastor of First Church of God. *(see page 54)*

William E. Ferguson and his wife Deb live in Takoma Park, Maryland. He is Senior Pastor of National Memorial Church of God in Washington, D.C. *(see page 60)*

Arthur F. Fleser is retired and lives in Wilmore, Kentucky. He is the former Chairman of the Divison of Speech Communication and English at Asbury College. Dr. Fleser has also taught at Geneva College in Beaver Falls, Pennsylvania. *(see page 64)*

Kenneth L. Gill lives in Longboat Key, Florida. He is Senior Pastor of Longboat Key Community Church. He has also pastored in Indiana and California. *(see page 66)*

Carole Pistole Greenwalt and her husband Ed live in Anderson, Indiana. She is an elementary school teacher and was on the staff at Anderson University in the Development Office. *(see page 56)*

Dwight L. Grubbs and his wife Sylvia live in Anderson, Indiana. He is an Associate Minister at Park Place Church of God and a former professor of Pastoral Care at Anderson School of Theology. *(see page 72)*

Jerry C. Grubbs and his wife Jan live in Anderson, Indiana. Dr. Grubbs was Dean of Chapel at Anderson University. He also served as Vice President for Student Affairs and Dean of Anderson School of Theology. *(see page 220)*

Sylvia Kennedy Grubbs and her husband Dwight live in Anderson, Indiana. She is a watercolor artist and is an Associate Minister at Park Place Church of God. *(see page 78)*

Arlene Smith Hall and her husband Ken live in Anderson, Indiana. She is the author of several books on Christian Education and Minister of Christian Education Emeritus at Park Place Church of God. *(see page 82)*

Kenneth F. Hall and his wife Arlene live in Anderson, Indiana. He is the author of several books and was Editor of Curriculum at Warner Press and a former Christian Education professor at Anderson University. *(see page 82)*

Ronald O. Hall and his wife Maxine live in Hartselle, Alabama. He retired as an engineer from the space industry in Huntsville, Alabama. *(see page 110)*

Michael A.V. Hamm and his wife Rhonda live in Anderson, Indiana. Dr. Hamm is Pastoral Counselor for Community VNA Hospice in Indianapolis, Indiana. *(see page 68)*

Daniel C. Harman and his wife Betty live in Anderson, Indiana. He is an ordained minister in the Church of God and the author of four books. He also served nine years as editor with Warner Press. *(see page 84)*

Madelyn Taylor Hartman lives in Anderson, Indiana. She and her late husband, Marvin Hartman, organized the Church of God in London, England. She is a writer, speaker and has led sessions for pastor's wives during the International Convention of the Church of God. *(see page 112)*

Sherrill D. Hayes and his wife Phyllis live in Lake Wales, Florida. He is the former Executive Secretary of the National Board of Christian Education of the Church of God. Dr. Hayes is an ordained minister in the Church of God and is now teaching at Warner Southern College. *(see page 88)*

John A. Howard and his wife Nancy live in Camrose, Alberta, Canada. He is the Chief Operations Officer and Dean of Faculty at Gardner College. *(see page 92)*

Suzanne Gaither Jennings and her husband Barry live near Alexandria, Indiana. She is a writer, songwriter and the mother of two. *(see page 94)*

Betty Jo Hyman Johnson and her husband Don live in Anderson, Indiana. She is a former missionary in Guyana and a pastor's wife. Betty Jo was an elementary school teacher. *(see page 98)*

Donald D. Johnson and his wife Betty Jo live in Anderson, Indiana. He is the former Executive Director of the Missionary Board of the Church of God. Dr. Johnson was a missionary in Guyana and was Senior Pastor of Park Place Church of God. *(see page 102)*

John M. Johnson and his wife Gwen live in Beirut, Lebanon. He is President of Mediterranean Bible College and pastor of Beirut International Church. *(see page 106)*

Arthur M. Kelly and his wife Judy live in Anderson, Indiana. He is the Coordinator of Publications for Church of God Ministries. Arthur was formerly the Dean at Warner Pacific College in Portland, Oregon. *(see page 100)*

Phyllis Gillespie Kinley and her husband Philip are retired and live in Anderson, Indiana. They served as missionaries in Japan for forty-three years. Both Phyllis and Philip are ministers in the Church of God. *(see page 222)*

Dale D. Landis and his wife Bonnie live in Pendleton, Indiana. He is Minister of Music at South Meridian Church of God in Anderson, Indiana. *(see page 104)*

David L. Lawson and his wife Paula live in Anderson, Indiana. Dr. Lawson is a former Director of World Service for the Church of God. *(see page 114)*

L. David Lewis and his wife Margaret live in Anderson, Indiana. Dr. Lewis was the Director of Liberal Arts Education at Anderson University and is presently the President and CEO of Overseas Council International in Greenwood, Indiana. *(see page 110)*

John W. Little and his wife Betty live in Anderson, Indiana. He is an ordained minister in the Church of God and a former Editor of Adult *Bridges* Curriculum. He has pastored congregations in Wisconsin, Indiana, Iowa and Michigan. *(see page 224)*

Avis Kleis Liverett and her husband David live in Anderson, Indiana. She was an elementary teacher both in Marion, Indiana, and in Anderson, Indiana. Avis works as office manager for D. Liverett Graphics. *(see page 118)*

James D. Lyon and his wife Maureen live in Anderson, Indiana. He is Senior Pastor of North Anderson Church of God and speaker for *ViewPoint*, CBH-English radio broadcast for Mass Media, Church of God Ministries. He was Senior Pastor of Fairview Church of God in Seattle, Washington, and a member of the Washington State House of Representatives. *(see page 200)*

James Earl Massey and his wife Gwendolyn live in Greensboro, Alabama. He is the author of several books and an ordained minister in the Church of God. Dr. Massey was Dean of Chapel at Tuskegee University. He served as Campus Minister at Anderson University and Dean of the School of Theology. He also was the speaker for the Christian Brotherhood Hour. *(see page 122)*

Joy L. May lives in Anderson, Indiana. She was a journalism major at Anderson University in Anderson, Indiana. Joy is the Senior Writer for Anderson University and does freelance editing for Thomas Nelson Publishers and Warner Press. *(see page 124)*

Robert I. Mathis and his wife Margaret live in Columbus, Ohio. He is an Associate Minister at Meadow Park Church of God. Bob has also served as Senior Pastor for congregations in Colorado and Pennsylvania. *(see page 130)*

Holly Gooding Miller and her husband Phil live in Anderson, Indiana. She is a Staff Writer for *The Saturday Evening Post* and *Today's Christian Woman*. Holly is a professor in the Communications Department at Anderson University. *(see page 132)*

Milo D. Miller and his wife Mona live in Casper, Wyoming. He is the Executive Pastor at Highland Park Church of God. Milo has served as Senior Pastor for congregations in Indiana, Florida and California. *(see page 144)*

T. Franklin Miller and his wife Gertie live in Anderson, Indiana. He is the author of several books and is a minister in the Church of God. Dr. Miller is a former Executive Secretary of the Board of Christian Education of the Church of God and President of Warner Press. *(see page 20 & 126)*

Charles N. Moore and his wife Elizabeth live in Clearwater, Florida. He is an ordained minister in the Church of God and has pastored in Tennessee, Alabama, California and Ohio. He has also been a probation officer. *(see page 196)*

James O. Morehead and his wife Jean live in Anderson, Indiana. He is the Senior Pastor of Pasadena Heights Church of God in Indianapolis, Indiana, and Associate Professor of Communications at Anderson University. *(see page 228)*

Jean Tolliver Morehead and her husband James live in Anderson, Indiana. She is the Associate Pastor of Pasadena Heights Church of God, Indianapolis, Indiana. Jean is also a Marriage and Family therapist, writer, seminar leader and motivational speaker. *(see page 208)*

Leslie H. Mosier and his wife Joyce live in Franklin, Tennessee. He retired as a chaplain in the U.S. Air Force with a rank of Lt. Col. *(see page 74)*

Eugene W. Newberry and his wife Agnes live in Anderson, Indiana. He is an ordained minister in the Church of God and former Dean of Anderson School of Theology. Dr. Newberry has authored four books. *(see page 128)*

Arlo F. Newell and his wife Helen live in Anderson, Indiana. He is an ordained minister in the Church of God and the former Editor-in-Chief of Warner Press. Dr. Newell is the author of five books and has pastored in Indiana, North Carolina, Missouri and Ohio. *(see page 134)*

Helen Jones Newell and her husband Arlo live in Anderson, Indiana. She taught Bible and Religion at Anderson University and has written adult curriculum for Warner Press. *(see page 138)*

Robert A. Nicholson and his wife Dorothy live in Anderson, Indiana. He is the former Dean of Anderson University and was the University's third President. Dr. Nicholson was the founder of the Anderson College Choir. *(see page 130)*

Richard H. Petersen and his wife Barbara live in Scarborough, Maine. Dr. Petersen is the founding Senior Pastor of Christ Church in Portland, Maine, and was the Director of the American Bible Society of Maine. *(see page 212)*

Harold L. Phillips lives in Anderson, Indiana. He is the former Editor-in-Chief of Warner Press and was a Bible professor at Anderson School of Theology. Dr. Phillips has authored several books. *(see page 142)*

Hollis S. Pistole and his wife Elizabeth live in Anderson, Indiana. He is an ordained minister in the Church of God and was a professor at Anderson School of Theology. He has pastored congregations in Ohio and Maryland. *(see page 146)*

Elizabeth Smith Pistole and her husband Hollis live in Anderson, Indiana. She has authored seven books and is a former secondary school teacher. *(see page 146)*

Robert H. Reardon and his wife Geraldine live in Anderson, Indiana. He was the second President of Anderson University and is a minister in the Church of God. Dr. Reardon has authored several books. *(see page 148)*

Hillery C. Rice was Senior Pastor of Park Place Church of God for ten years. He also pastored churches in West Virginia and Florida. Dr. Rice worked in the Development Office at Anderson University into his nineties. He has written four books about the Church of God. *(see page 150)*

W. Malcolm Rigel and his wife Martha live in Lake Wales, Florida. He is an ordained minister in the Church of God and a song writer. Dr. Rigel is presently associated with Warner Southern College. *(see page 38)*

Frederick G. Shackleton and his wife Doris live in Anza, California. He is an ordained minister in the Church of God and has pastored five congregations. He has taught at Anderson University, Warner Pacific College and Azusa Pacific University. He was written hymns, church school curriculum, and one book, *Toward a Living Hope*. *(see page 218)*

Fredrick H. Shively and his wife Kay live in Anderson, Indiana. He is an ordained minister in the Church of God and a Professor of Bible and Religion at Anderson University. He has pastored congregations in California and Oregon. *(see page 154)*

Kay Murphy Shively and her husband Fred live in Anderson, Indiana. She is a writer and former teacher and was most recently a program coordinator for WOMEN OF THE CHURCH OF GOD. *(see page 204)*

Charles R. Shumate and his wife Laretta live in Anderson, Indiana. Dr. Shumate is an ordained minister in the Church of God and an associate with the Board of Church Extension of the Church of God. *(see page 150)*

David G. Singer and his wife *Risë Wood Singer* live in Pendleton, Indiana. He is a retired Engineering Manager from General Motors. He is now a professional wood carver. Risë is retired from working in the legal field. David and Risë travel extensively. Both are lighthouse enthusiasts. *(see page 198)*

Janetta Hitt Slattery and her husband Philip live in Anderson, Indiana. She is a high school English teacher. *(see page 160)*

Ann Espey Smith and her husband Nathan live in Anderson, Indiana. She was the interim Senior Pastor at Park Place Church of God. Dr. Smith was a missionary to Japan and Korea and an associate with the Missionary Board of the Church of God. *(see page 162)*

Caroline Melton Smith and her husband Jack live in Anderson, Indiana, and in Naples, Florida. She is a writer and a former editor of the youth magazine, *Between Times*, for Warner Press. *(see page 160)*

Billie Roy Smith lives in Huntsville, Alabama. He is a writer, an ordained minister in the Church of God, and a retired Certified Public Accountant. *(see page 164)*

Roscoe Snowden and his wife Nellie live in Anderson, Indiana. He is an ordained minister in the Church of God and the former Director of Church Service for the Church of God. *(see page 24)*

Leonard W. Snyder and his wife Jean live in Delaware, Ohio. He is an ordained minister in the Church of God and was Senior Pastor at First Church of God in Hamilton, Ohio. He was Ohio State Cooridinator for the Church of God. *(see page 168)*

James L. Sparks and his wife Susan live in Battle Creek, Michigan. He is Senior Pastor of North Avenue Church of God. *(see page 170)*

Sue Miller Spaulding and her husband Spencer live in Anderson, Indiana. She is an English professor at Anderson University. *(see page 180)*

Gilbert W. Stafford and his wife Darlene live in Anderson, Indiana. He is an ordained minister in the Church of God and a former speaker for the Christian Brotherhood Hour. Dr. Stafford is a professor of Christian Theology and Dean of Chapel at Anderson School of Theology. He is the author of several books. *(see page 58)*

Christie Smith Stephens and her husband Stan live in Anderson, Indiana. She is a writer and an advocate for survivors of domestic and sexual abuse/violence. Christie co-founded Women's Alternatives, Inc., a social service agency. She and David Liverett collaborated on the book *Oh, to be in Miss Collier's class again! (see pages 14, 28, 42, 62, 76, 90, 108, 120, 140, 158, 176, 202, 210, 216, 226, & 229)*

R. Eugene Sterner and his wife Millie live in Anderson, Indiana. Dr. Sterner is an ordained minister in the Church of God and a former speaker for the Christian Brotherhood Hour. *(see page 178)*

Merle D. Strege and his wife Fran live in Anderson, Indiana. He is a Bible professor at Anderson University and has written several books about the early history of the Church of God. Dr. Strege is the Church of God Historian. *(see page 182)*

Paul A. Tanner and his wife Jean live in Anderson, Indiana. He is a former Director of World Service and was Executive Director of the Executive Council of the Church of God. *(see page 184)*

Joyce Thompson Thornton and her husband Carl live in Killen, Alabama. She was an administrative assistant with AEtna Life and Casualty in Florence, Alabama. *(see page 214)*

Bethany K. Warner is from Canton, Ohio, and as a student at Anderson University was an intern with the American Studies Program in Washington, D.C. She has written for the *Washington Times*. *(see page 186)*

Gibb E. Webber and his wife Georiga live in Anderson, Indiana. He is a retired English professor at Anderson University. *(see page 188)*

William A. White and his wife Pam live in Anderson, Indiana. He is Editor of Adult *Bridges* Curriculum of the Church of God. Bill also edits *Pathways to God*. *(see page 190)*

Richard L. Willowby and his wife Cheryl live in Anderson, Indiana. He is Senior Pastor at Hope Community Church of God in Clarksville, Indiana. Richard is the former Managing Editor of *Vital Christianity*. (see page 195)

Oral Withrow and his wife Laura live in Anderson, Indiana, and Phoenix, Arizona. He was the assistant to the President of the Missionary Board of the Church of God. Presently he is the assistant to the Senior Pastor at Mountain Park Community Church in Phoenix. Dr. Withrow was Senior Pastor for congregations of the Church of God in Ohio, Missouri and Wyoming. *(see page 174)*

Anita Smith Womack (1937-2000) was Director of Head Start in Anderson, Indiana, and later Director of the Children's Center at Park Place Church of God. She served as Minister of Christian Education at Park Place from 1989 to 1998. *(see page 86)*

Joe K. Womack is retired and lives in Anderson, Indiana, and in Bradenton, Florida. Joe was Director of the Social Work Program at Anderson University. *(see page 36)*

Lighthouses

Matted prints and packets of ten notecards with envelopes of any lighthouse,
may be ordered by using the identification number listed for the lighthouse.
(Example: MI1001 identifies Big Sable Point near Ludington, MI).
Chinaberry House • PO Box 505 • Anderson, Indiana 46015 • 765-644-2492
Email: dliverett@aol.com • www.2lights.com